A Plant-Based Lifestyle
For You And The Planet

I0532382

Sharon Leontine Wallenberg

Liberty 61 Books, Inc.

Library of Congress

ISN: 979-8-9882618-4-1

Liberty 61 Books, Inc.

Dedication:

This book is dedicated to all the countless individuals, of all species, who have suffered from injustice.

"Blessed are those who hunger and thirst for JUSTICE. They will be satisfied." The Beatitudes.

Introduction

Today everyone is concerned with health, quality of life, and longevity. Old ways are not working, and it is becoming more obvious that a comprehensive new approach is necessary. No longer can we wait unit illness occurs or incorporate a nominal amount of exercise and supplements into our regime and consider the problem solved. What is needed is a new Lifestyle! And one that works!

Preventative medicine is a relatively new concept. Given the rising healthcare costs, and plethora of preventable illness, it has practical ramifications. Preventative medicine involves diet and exercise to prevent the more egregious and expensive maladies and for practical reasons and is beginning to have roots in modern medicine. Lifestyle Medicine has begun to emerge as an alternative to conventional ways that are not working.

I think it is possible to go further than preventative medicine and lifestyle medicine to simply 'lifestyle' which encompasses all facets of living life. It is physical, mental and spiritual – mind, body, and soul! This concept has been around for many years and was considered 'new age'. Although its roots may have been on the fringe, it is finally becoming a main-stream concept. Doctors may refer to it as 'Lifestyle Medicine', but I prefer to simply call it 'Lifestyle' since it is an all-encompassing healthy way to live life.

'Lifestyle' includes not only Diet and Exercise, but also Relaxation, Rejuvenation, Detox, Happiness, Kindness, Compassion, Courage, Humility, Gratitude and Honesty - and most importantly - Forgiveness. A toxic, unforgiving lifestyle can lead just as easily to disease and debilitation as any tangible cause. Happiness and kindness may not have monetary value or scientific studies to prove their worth, but I believe they contribute greatly to wholesomeness and longevity.

This book proposes to show you how you can live a fuller life, without the assortment of contemporary illness, dissatisfactions, and emptiness, a life that includes not just health, but happiness and purpose. One that is lived with courage and conviction, is meaningful and enjoyable and includes the satisfaction of knowing that your life makes a difference for many more besides yourself. It is called the Plant-Based (Vegan) Lifestyle.

The Plant-Based (Vegan) Lifestyle is about compassion. It is not just a diet. It is a Lifestyle that not only involves diet, exercise, and health. It is about making the world a better place, not only for people, but for the billions of other inhabitants we share this planet with. It is about providing simple solutions to complex global issues.

Plant-based (vegan) is not a form of deprivation. It is a lifestyle which embraces life, and life lived to the fullest. This lifestyle holds the promise of a healthier population, a sustainable planet, and kindness and compassion for all.

The plant-based lifestyle concept involves more than just eating. It is all encompassing. It involves not only people, the planet, and our fellow travelers on spaceship Earth, but also the broader concepts of Peace, Prosperity for all, and Social Justice.

The meat and dairy based diet causes catastrophic health concerns - such as skyrocketing diabetes, cancer, heart disease, potentially devastating antibiotic resistance, along with accompanying rising health care costs. A plant-based diet is the best for optimal health – human, animal, and planet. It has been proven to prevent and reverse heart disease, prevent and treat cancer, and prevent and reverse diabetes, the three largest causes of mortality and morbidity in both men and women. In addition, it is globally sustainable. The meat and dairy based diet is not sustainable because of the vast amounts of water, grain, and land needed, and the pollution produced. Methane from animals raised for food traps heat in the atmosphere much more effectively than carbon dioxide, making it the single largest cause of global warming.

"The word 'vegan" was coined by Donald Watson, a British woodworker. Watson became a vegetarian at the age of 12 after seeing a pig slaughtered on his uncle's farm in Yorkshire, England. He and his wife Dorothy founded the Vegan Society in 1944. Looking for a name for a vegetarian diet that also excluded other animal products, he put together letters from the beginning and end of the word "vegetarian" to spell "vegan", a word now found in most dictionaries." From The Vegan Bible.

Vegan has ultimately evolved into a lifestyle which includes the plant-based diet, a cruelty free, human supremacy free philosophy, and a sustainable system of choices benefiting all on planet Earth, as well as the planet itself. In short, it is the key to happiness, health, and well-being for all.

Before you decide this is too 'extreme', I invite you to read the position of the

American Dietetic Association, which is the leading authority on Diet and Nutrition in the United States. As you can see, you have nothing to fear:

"It is the position of the American Dietetic Association that appropriately planned vegetarian diets, including total vegetarian or VEGAN DIETS, are healthful, nutritionally adequate, and may provide health benefits in the prevention and treatment of certain diseases. Well-planned vegetarian diets are appropriate for individuals during all stages of the life cycle, including pregnancy, lactation, infancy, childhood, and adolescence, and for athletes. A vegetarian diet is defined as one that does not include meat (including fowl) or seafood, or products containing those foods. This article reviews the current data related to key nutrients for vegetarian including protein, n-3 fatty acids, iron, zinc, iodine, calcium, and vitamins D and B-12. A vegetarian diet can meet current recommendation for all of these nutrients. In some cases, supplements or fortified foods can provide useful amounts of important nutrients. An evidence – based review showed that vegetarian diets can be nutritionally adequate in pregnancy and result in positive maternal and infant health outcomes. The results of an evidence-based review showed that a vegetarian diet is associated with a lower risk of death from ischemic heart disease. Vegetarians also appear to have lower low-density lipoprotein cholesterol levels, lower blood pressure, and lower rates of hypertension and type 2 diabetes than nonvegetarians. Furthermore, vegetarians tend to have a lower body mass index and lower overall cancer rates. Features of a vegetarian diet that may reduce risk of chronic disease include lower intakes of saturated fat and cholesterol and higher intakes of fruits, vegetables, whole grains, nuts, soy products, fiber, and phytochemicals. The variability of dietary practices among vegetarians makes individual assessment of dietary adequacy essential. In addition to assessing dietary adequacy, food and nutrition professional can also play key roles in educating vegetarians about sources of specific nutrients, food purchase and preparation, and dietary modification to meet their needs."

A Plant-Based (vegan) diet is one that contains no animal products - that is no meat, chicken, fish or shellfish. It does not contain any dairy products – no milk, cream, yogurt, cheese, or eggs. In addition, there is no honey; molasses is just as sweet, and contains B vitamins. A vegan diet is rich in fruit, salads, sprouts, nuts, berries, whole grains, tofu, meat substitutes like tofurkey, and other imaginative creations.

No living creatures are ever exploited in creating a plant-based vegan diet. The vegan diet is the most compassionate for all species. The raw food vegan diet is the most healthful of all diets because it is richest in fiber, vitamins and minerals, and it is vegan! There are specialty vegan bakeries, many vegan restaurants, and many restaurants offer vegan selections.

The term "Lifestyle Medicine" has come to mean a new way of life that includes not only prevention of illness but also those intangible assets which make a life worth living – happiness, courage, conviction, purpose. This is what Dean Ornish, M.D., a pioneer in the Lifestyle Medicine field, has to say:

"Our research … helped create the new field of lifestyle medicine – that is - using comprehensive lifestyle changes to treat and even reverse the progression of many of the most common chronic diseases, as well as to help prevent them. Our Genes Are Not Our Fate. I often hear people say, "Oh, its all in my genes. There's not much I can do about it." Fortunately, now we know that there is." "Dr. Dean Ornish's Program For Reversing Heart Disease", Dean Ornish, M.D.

A cancer specialist, Bernie Siegel, M.D., studied the concept of lifestyle medicine. He was intrigued by the fact that two patients can have the same diagnosis and one patient survives, while the other does not. Dr. Siegel decided to observe the lifestyles of his patients to see what was making this life or death the difference. He published his findings in "Love, Medicine and Miracles".

The United States has the most expensive health care in the world and, according to United Nations statistics - some of the least healthy people in the world. The food we eat is a big part of this dilemma. Cardiovascular disease, diabetes, obesity, and more, can be prevented and often reversed with a whole-foods, plant-based diet. Eating beans, grains, fruits and vegetables are both more healthful and more affordable than the processed foods, meat and dairy which are causing these diseases.

The lifestyle medicine concept involves not only treating disease and illness - but most importantly, living life in such a way that disease does not occur, or at least not as frequently or severely, and focusing on having a full, happy, healthy, and meaningful life.

In addition to the way we treat ourselves with diet, exercise, and proper values, it is all worthless unless we can project these values outward to the world around us.

What I am suggesting is that we go beyond ourselves to create a better world.

Yes, this involves the way we treat all our fellow travelers on spaceship Earth, as well as the way we treat the Earth herself. It is about not only what we eat, wear, use, etc., but how it was produced, and the political, corporate, and financial ramifications involved, as well as those who suffer or benefit from our decisions.

I wish you all good things in your new lifestyle!

Contents

Chapter 1 Nutrition 101 Protein, Carbohydrates, Fat, Fiber, Vitamins and Minerals

Food has three categories: Protein, Carbohydrates, and Fat. All three are essential for life. The human body also requires vitamins, minerals and fiber for optimal good health. The Whole Food Plant Based Diet contains all these without the unnecessary and harmful additional fat and cholesterol in the meat and dairy based diet.

Protein provides the functional and structural component of the human body and synthesis of hormones and neurotransmitters. Digestion breaks down protein into amino acids which are then used by the body. Amino acids are categorized as essential, conditionally essential, or nonessential. There are 22 amino acids, only eight of these amino acids are considered essential. They are: histidine, isoleucine, lysine, methionine, phenylalanine, threonine, tryptophan, valine, methionine, and phenylalanine. Amino acid arginine is considered essential when fighting cancer.

Essential amino acids are organic. In Chemistry, compounds that contain carbon, hydrogen, nitrogen, and oxygen are classified as organic, and those that do not contain carbon are classified as inorganic. Amino acids contain carbon, nitrogen, hydrogen, and oxygen, along with a variable side chain group.

Essential amino acids cannot be made by the body like the nonessential amino acids. They must be obtained by diet. Animal protein is a secondary source. It does not make any sense to get essential amino acids from a secondary source when the primary source – plants - are available. This is where the animals got the protein from. Plants are the best source of amino acids.

All of the essential amino acids are found in plants. There is sufficient protein in vegetables and fruit, especially in the traditional combination of grains and legumes – which contains all the essential amino acids. This combination is traditionally rice and beans or corn and lima beans. Most animals, such as the horse- one of the world's fastest animals, and the elephant – one of the world's strongest animals, eat grass and leaves which are rich in energy synthesized from the sun. Animals raised for food, such as cattle and chickens, also eat food rich in plant-based energy when they are fed properly.

Beans belong to a family of high-protein plant foods called legumes. They provide all nine essential amino acids except methionine. Grains are generally high in methionine, this includes rice, corn, oats, wheat, quinoa. Although different beans provide varying amounts of nutrients, they all contain a similar balance of essential amino acids. Grains are generally high in methionine and beans are a good sources of lysine. Black beans and kidney beans contain concentrations of all essential amino acids

This is what the experts say about protein:

"Myth: You Can't Get Enough Protein on a Vegan Diet. This myth will not die, despite 1) statements supporting vegan diets from major nutrition organizations, (2) the wealth of protein in beans, vegetables, and grains, (3) the massive musculature of rhinoceroses, elephants, and other vegan animals, and (4) the millions of people following vegan diets with no evidence that protein is an issue at all." Neal Barnard, M.D.

"The lie that you need to eat milk, eggs, or dead animals to get protein in your diet is the lie that has built up the factory farming and slaughterhouse industries into huge environmental travesties in which billions of animals live horrible lives and die horrible deaths – with many of them being cut into and dismembered while they are still alive."

"All fruits and vegetables contain the essential amino acids your body needs to make protein. You will get all of the amino acids you need by eating enough calories of fruits, vegetables, nuts, and seeds." John McCabe, Sunfood Traveler

"Nature designed and synthesized our foods complete with all the essential nutrients for human life long before they reach the dinner table. All the essential and nonessential amino acids are represented in single unrefined starches such as rice, corn, wheat, and potatoes in amounts in excess of every individual's needs, even if they are endurance athletes or weight-lifters." John A. McDougall, M.D. "The McDougal Program"

Carbohydrates are found in plants: vegetables, fruit, grains, and legumes, and are the source of energy for the body.

All energy comes from the sun. Chlorophyll, the green color in plants is responsible for absorption of light from the sun which is used for a process called photosynthesis. This is the process by which green plants and other organisms convert light energy from the sun into chemical energy that can later be released as fuel for the organism's activities. This process synthesizes foods from carbon dioxide and water, generates oxygen as a by-product, and is the basis of food energy. Carbohydrates made by plants are stored in their leaves, stems, roots, fruits, and in whole grains, tubers, and legumes,

The so called 'bad carbs' refers to processed foods. These are foods in boxes and bags which have been stripped of their protein, fiber, vitamins and minerals. These are also called 'empty calories' because processed food contains calories, but none of the other necessary nutrients. All food in a box or a bag is processed. Unprocessed food comes from fields and trees.

There are many myths about carbohydrate. Some people choose to avoid gluten, the protein found in wheat. Only one person in a hundred has celiac, the allergy to gluten.

"Myth: Carbohydrates Are Fattening…carbohydrates have only 4 calories per gram, compared with 9 for fats and oils. People blame carbs for weight gain that comes from eating cakes and cookies." Neal Barnard, M.D.

Fat is a form of energy storage for an individual's use in the event of a food shortage. It is not used unless there is food insecurity. Cholesterol is a waxy substance produced by non-plants (humans and other sentient beings) for use in their body for cell repairs, and other functions. The human body produces enough of its own cholesterol for these purposes.

Additional fat and cholesterol in the body resulting from the meat and dairy based diet clogs arteries causing heart disease; fills cells so they cannot accept glucose for energy causing diabetes; and is also considered to be responsible for some cancers. The most healthful diet is the cholesterol free, whole food, plant based vegan diet.

According to Neal Barnard, M.D. in "The Vegan Starter Kit": "Animal products drive cholesterol levels skyward. First of all, meat, dairy products, and eggs contain cholesterol – with eggs at the top of the list- and roughly half of the cholesterol you eat ends up in your bloodstream. Much worse is the saturated ("bad") fat in dairy products, meat and eggs. It stimulates your body to make extra cholesterol. Plants are just the opposite. They have very little saturated fat and are essentially cholesterol free."

Fiber is essential for optimal health. Fiber transports toxins out of the body through the colon. Without fiber, toxins remain in the colon where they putrefy. The uneliminated toxins are reabsorbed through the villi of the intestine directly into the blood stream. Then they circulate to every part of the body and poison it.

Dietary fiber is found only in the whole food plant-based diet. Fruit, vegetables, seeds, nuts, grains and legumes are nutrient dense, high in fiber, and provide an excellent source of vitamins, minerals and protein. Fiber not only aids in elimination of toxins, but also improves cholesterol levels, lowers blood sugar levels and aids in weight loss or weight management.

Vitamins are organic – they contain carbon, hydrogen, oxygen and nitrogen. They are synthesized by plants and bacteria. People can make their own Vitamin D from sunlight. Some vitamins come from human bowel activity. There are sufficient vitamins in the Plant Based diet to make vitamin supplements unnecessary.

Minerals are inorganic; they do not contain carbon and come from the earth. Plants absorb them through their roots and store them in their roots, stalks, leaves and fruit.

Vitamins and minerals come mostly from soil directly, not through animals. Vitamins, both the fat-soluble vitamins A, D, and K, and water-soluble vitamins B and C, as well as minerals, are readily available in a varied plant-based diet. Using animals as a source of vitamins and minerals for humans is essentially obtaining the vitamins and minerals second hand from the prematurely deceased individual who originally received the vitamins and minerals from plants. Eating a varied plant-based diet makes taking supplements unnecessary.

Vitamin D comes from sunshine and can overcome depression without the need for medication. It is a scientific fact that sunshine produces a chemical reaction in the brain. The brain produces serotonin, a chemical that is a potent mood enhancer. There is a relationship between serotonin production and bright light, usually the sun, but it can also be from artificial light. Serotonin is a natural anti-depressant without the dangerous side effects of antidepressant drugs. Some of these drugs have been linked to suicides. Conversely, the lack of sunshine has been scientifically proven to cause depression. People who spend most of their time indoors not only miss receiving Vitamin D from the action of sunlight on the skin, but also have a higher risk of depression.

All fruits and vegetables contain vitamins and minerals. They are especially plentiful when produce is grown sustainably. Minerals come from the soil. Most vitamins are synthesized in plants, and some, specifically vitamin D, is synthesized in the human bodies.

If soil is repeatedly planted, it becomes depleted of minerals and there are fewer nutrients in the produce. The evidence of this is the lack of flavor and taste in produce. Sustainable or veganic agriculture allows soil to replenish by using nitrogen rich cover crops and plowing them under to replenish soil. This is not done in either conventional or organic agriculture.

During photosynthesis, the process used by plants to convert light energy from the sun into chemical energy, vitamins, carbohydrates, amino acids (the building blocks of proteins), lipids (fats), pigments, and other components of green tissues are synthesized. Minerals supply the elements of nitrogen, phosphorus, sulfur, required to form these compounds. Plants synthesize a wide range of vitamins that are essential for humans. Unlike the other vitamins, Vitamin D comes from the sun and is synthesized in the human body.

A good way to know if there is an ample supply of vitamins and minerals in your diet is to eat fruits and vegetables of a variety of colors. This will insure you are receiving lots of vitamins and minerals.

Green fruits and vegetables contain Vitamins A, C, E, K, B 6, calcium, magnesium, and iron. Vegetables: spinach, kale, broccoli, asparagus, peas, avocado, brussels sprouts, cabbage, celery. Fruits: honey dew melon, limes, green apples, green grapes.

Orange and yellow fruits and vegetables contain Vitamins A, C, K, potassium, which regulates blood pressure, and folate. Vegetables: carrots, sweet potatoes, pumpkin, butternut squash, corn, orange and yellow peppers. Fruits: oranges, grapefruit, bananas, apricot, nectarines, peaches, cantaloupe, pineapple, papaya.

Red fruits and vegetables contain Vitamins A, C, and potassium. Vegetables: tomatoes, beets, red peppers, red onions, red cabbage, radishes. Fruits: cherries, strawberries, watermelon, apples, raspberries.

Purple fruits and vegetables contain manganese, Vitamins K, C potassium, and B Vitamins. Vegetables; eggplant, purple sweet potatoes, purple cauliflower, beets, red cabbage. Fruits: plums, blackberries.

Blue fruits and vegetables contain antioxidants and phytonutrients which decrease inflammation, minerals including copper and iron, and vitamins C, K, B-6, B-12. Vegetables: blue corn, blue potatoes. Fruit: blueberries, concord grapes.

White fruits and vegetables contain vitamin C and potassium. Vegetables: mushrooms, cucumber, onions, cauliflower, potatoes. Fruits: pears, coconut.

Sprouts of all kinds are especially full of vitamins, minerals and nutrients.

Here are other sources of vitamins and minerals from "The Vegan Starter Kit" by Neal Barnard, M.D.:

Calcium

"Where do you get calcium without dairy products? Well, cows don't actually make calcium at all. Calcium comes from the Earth. Green vegetables pull calcium from the soil through their roots, and it ends up in their leaves. When cows eat grass, calcium passes into their milk."

Iron

"You need iron to make the hemoglobin that your blood cells use to transport oxygen, and the best sources are green leafy vegetables and beans. In fact, in our research studies, people adopting a vegan diet often get slightly more iron than they did on a meatand-dairy diet, thanks to the iron in greens and beans."

Vitamin B12

"Vitamin B12 is essential for healthy nerves and healthy blood cells. But it is not made by plants or animals. It is made by bacteria. Some people speculate that before the advent of modern hygiene, the traces of bacteria in the soil, on vegetables, on our fingers, and in our mouths gave us the traces of B12 we needed. Whether that is true or not, modern hygiene has eliminated that possibility."

Vitamin D

"Vitamin D is produced by sunlight on your skin. It helps you absorb calcium from the foods you eat and also helps protect against cancer. About 20 minutes of sunlight on your face and arms a few times each week gives you the vitamin D you need."

Omega 3s

"Although some fats are risky – saturated fats raise cholesterol, for example – your body does need traces of good fats. One in particular is called ALA, or alpha-linolenic acid. The name is not important, though what is important is that it is a healthful omega-3 fatty acid that your body will lengthen into another omega-3, called DHA (docosahexaenoic acid), that your brain uses. Where do you find it? There are ALA traces in leafy vegetables, fruits, and beans, and much larger amounts in walnuts and various seeds."

Vitamins

"For most people, there is no need for a multivitamin or other vitamin supplements (unless your caregiver has specifically called for them)."

These are the new Four Food Groups: Whole Grains, Legumes, Vegetables, Fruit.

Whole Grains: Brown rice, oats, barley, corn, products: bread, cereals, pasta, etc.

Legumes: Beans, peas, lentils, soy products, veggie burgers, meatless hot dogs, vegan deli slices, tofurky, etc.

Vegetables: It is best to choose a variety of colors for different benefits.

Fruit: A variety of seasonal fruit is best.

For complete nutrition and optimal health eat a variety of vegetables, fruits, whole grains, and legumes and maintain a whole food plant-based diet!

Chapter 2 Digestion

The Digestive System processes everything that is eaten by breaking it down into smaller and smaller pieces and mixing it with digestive enzymes until nourishment is absorbed directly into the blood stream and travels to all cells of the body to nourish them. The Digestive System includes the mouth, teeth, esophagus, stomach, small intestine, large intestine and rectum.

When the body is low on nutrients, the stomach releases the hormone ghrelin to send a signal to the brain. This and also thoughts, sights and smells of food begin the salivary process. Three pair of salivary glands in the cheeks and under the jaw and tongue release saliva. These three pair of salivary glands secrete about a quart and a half of fluid saliva daily into the mouth. Sufficient daily intake of water is essential for healthy, efficient digestion. Saliva contains the enzyme amylase which breaks down carbohydrate -starch – into a sugar called maltose.

Teeth chew the food into smaller and smaller pieces in the mouth stimulating more saliva flow. Next, food goes through the esophagus into the stomach. Peristalsis is the process of moving food through the digestive system. There are two layers of smooth muscle – lengthwise and in rings which contract rhythmically to push food through the esophagus and through the entire digestive system.

Swallowing causes pressure on a sphincter muscle at the top of the esophagus to relax and let food through. Once the food has entered the esophagus, peristalsis causes the muscles to contract and relax in sequence, moving the food through. At the lower end of the esophagus, the cardiac sphincter relaxes and opens into the stomach. The food in the stomach cannot go back into esophagus because of one way valve called the pyloric valve.

Digestion in the stomach takes about 4 hours. Gastric chief cells in the stomach secrete pepsin as an inactive zymogen called pepsinogen. Pepsin breaks down protein. In addition to digesting protein, the stomach secretes hydrochloric acid, and extremely powerful acid, to kill any harmful bacteria or microbes. Food is reduced to a creamy liquid in the stomach.

Last, the food enters the intestines by traveling through the pyloric sphincter into the small intestine. Most of the digestion is done in the small intestine. The pancreas which secretes insulin also secretes an alkaline solution into the small intestine to neutralize the hydrochloric stomach acid. The pancreas produces insulin as well as digestive fluids. Pancreatic digestive fluids contain many enzymes that digest protein, carbohydrate, and fat. The duodenum secretes bile from the liver. Bile is a fluid that is made and released by the liver and stored in the gallbladder. Bile breaks down fat globules by emulsifying them and turning them into thousands of tiny droplets of fatty acids which are stored as a source of energy for the body. The liver, pancreas, and gallbladder all produce and store enzymes used in the digestive process.

In the small intestine, food is digested into small molecules. The end products of digestion are single molecules of glucose (simple sugar) which are absorbed into the blood stream directly through the villi (small finger like projections) in the intestine. These villi are covered with even smaller villi called microvilli. Inside each villus (singular of villi) is a network of blood vessels called capillaries with very thin walls which pick up small molecules of digested food. This nourishment enters directly into the bloodstream and circulates throughout the body. These single molecules of glucose (simple sugar) are taken to every cell in the body to provide nourishment. If the glucose cannot enter the cells to provide nourishment due to congestion in the cell from excessive fat and cholesterol, this simple sugar remains in the bloodstream causing a symptom of diabetes.

Digested food travels through the bloodstream to the liver where the concentrations of sugar, amino acids, and other substances are kept in balance. The liver filters and flushes out toxic substances, such as pollutants, bacterial toxins, and chemicals. The liver also destroys poisons including alcohol and it manufactures vitamin A. The liver removes bacteria, debris, and old red blood cells from the blood and breaks down worn out cells converting them into bile. The liver accumulates nutrients, primarily vitamins, minerals, and glycogen, a form of stored glucose. When the body needs energy, the liver converts glycogen into glucose and sends it into the blood.

The remaining undigested food enters the large intestine. The water from this mass is absorbed from the intestine leaving behind a semisolid material. Good bacteria in the intestines are called probiotics and are necessary for good health. They secrete vitamins including vitamin K. Harmless bacteria feed on the waste matter and break down some of the fiber releasing sugar and some vitamins which are absorbed by the body. These bacteria produce methane and carbon dioxide which are greenhouse gasses. These gasses from the billions of animals raised for food are a significant contributor to global warming. Waste can remain in the large intestine for days or longer if there is not sufficient water and fiber for efficient elimination.

Feces, the final remaining digestive waste, is eliminated from the colon through the rectum. This toxic waste needs fiber for bulk and water for lubrication to facilitate elimination. If the toxic end products of digestion are not eliminated, they are reabsorbed directly into the bloodstream, and poison every cell in the body.

When you have eaten enough, fat tissues in your body release the hormone leptin which signals your brain to reduce the appetite.

It takes about 48 hours for food to pass through the human body.

Water is necessary for digestion to make the digestive enzymes and hydrochloric acid to kill harmful bacteria, and to aid in elimination.

The plant-based diet provides all the nutrients, vitamins and minerals, as well as the fiber needed to eliminate waste, without the hormones, fat, cholesterol, antibiotics, and hormones prevalent in the meat and dairy based diet.

Chapter 3 Raw Food

What is raw food? It is food which has not been cooked leaving all the vitamins, minerals, and nutrients still whole and intact. Raw food is most commonly found in salads, raw fruit, uncooked vegetables - often referred to as crudites. Your grapefruit with breakfast, side salad with lunch, and uncooked vegetables at dinner all count! Many people choose to eat all their food raw. This gives the health benefits of as many vitamins, and minerals and as much fiber as possible in their diet for optimal health benefits.

Cooking food destroys bacteria, which is important. There are many potentially fatal diseases caused by microorganisms. One very deadly disease is Botulism. This anerobic (needs no air) bacteria can cause human fatalities. There is no cure. Yes, it is the same one used for beauty purposes, and yes, there is an occasional fatality. Cooking food to prevent contamination by disease causing bacteria and other microorganisms is one of the original purposes for this treatment of food. However, in addition to preventing food borne disease, it also destroys the vitamins and minerals needed for optimal health.

What a quandary! Do we want the good health provided by the vitamins and minerals, or do we want to be safe from food borne pathogens?

The answer is we want both. The goal is to avoid potentially contaminated food and eat as much healthful raw, uncooked foods as possible. Since many pathogens come from the abusive, exploitive, profit seeking treatment of innocent animals, we will want to avoid conventionally farmed produce which may have been exposed to Escherichia coli. E. coli is a bacteria found in the colon of all sentient beings which is essential to their digestive system but harmful when ingested by someone else. Samonella is another similar dangerous bacteria. Eating organic produce will not solve this problem. It will only expose you to 'organic' pathogens. This means pathogens from animals which have been fed an 'organic' diet and slaughtered on Monday after the murder machines were cleaned over the weekend, as opposed to being murdered during the other weekdays. Does that make it worth the extra money? It is up to you.

Veganic agriculture uses no animal inputs and is the only way to be sure that the raw food you are eating to receive all the health benefits is without the potential for disease.

Eating veganic raw foods is the optimal way to safe, vibrant health.

Stay healthy! Eat raw, veganic fruits, vegetables and salads!

Chapter 4 Water

Water is extremely necessary for life. No one can live without water. The human body is more than 50 percent water and can be from 60 to 70 percent water depending on the individual. The entire human body needs water to function. Water is used in every system and function in the body.

For many reasons water is an essential element for life. It is not just a passive solvent in which salts, compounds, and gasses interact; water participates actively in forming building blocks of cells and is the environment in which cells live.

Starting at conception, the human body needs water. Mother's morning sickness is caused by the water needs of her baby. As the baby develops, the surrounding water increases. This embryonic water is taken from the Mother's water supply. Morning sickness indicates that additional water is needed to support the needs of the baby.

Dry crackers will not solve the problem. Morning sickness requires additional water intake.

Energy generation requires water. The osmotic flow of water through membranes generates 'hydroelectric' energy (voltage). This is converted and stored as ATP and GTP - chemical sources of energy in the body.

The human body's nervous system needs water to function. Impulses (messages) from the brain are conducted through the nervous system. These impulses jump between nerve cells across small synapses filled with water. Dehydration can slow or stop nerve impulses from reaching their destination in the body. In order for the brain to transmit impulses to the rest of the body effectively, there needs to be sufficient water to fill these synapses.

Immune system suppression is a direct result of dehydration. The proper functioning of the immune system depends on nutrients in the blood stream. If there is insufficient water resulting from dehydration or chronic dehydration, these nutrients cannot be properly transported to the destination organ or system.

Chronic pains, not easily explained as injury or infection, can be interpreted as signals of chronic water shortage in the painful area. This includes dyspeptic pain (heartburn), rheumatoid arthritis pain, low back pain, migraine and hangover headaches, colitis pain, and associated constipation.

Water is needed for digestion. It is the major ingredient in all digestive enzymes and is necessary for food to be in the semiliquid state required for digestion. Peristalsis – the rhythmic muscle contractions that move food through the digestive system – cannot occur without water.

Heartburn is caused by dehydration. The innermost lining of the stomach is covered with mucosa. Mucosa is 98% water, similar to a sponge. This 'water layer' is a natural buffer between the stomach and the hydrochloride acid secreted to kill any bacteria in the food being digested. If there is not enough water to fill the mucosa, it becomes like a compressed dry sponge. When the body is dehydrated, the stomach lining cannot provide a barrier between the stomach and the HCl. The result is heartburn. Some acid may flow into the esophagus when a person is lying down which can also cause 'heartburn'. Commercial antacid remedies contain aluminum which can be deadly.

Blood sugar is regulated by the pancreas. The pancreas also secretes an alkaline watery bicarbonate solution to neutralize the acid entering the intestine from the stomach. To manufacture this watery, bicarbonate solution, the pancreas needs copious amounts of water. If the pancreas cannot produce this solution due to dehydration, the pyloric valve between the stomach and the intestine will not open and allow the acidic stomach contents to enter the intestines. The digestive products will remain in the stomach, further exacerbating the acidic problem and causing 'heartburn'. This will also cause problems in regulating blood sugar because in times of dehydration, all functions of the pancreas are compromised.

Constipation has many causes, including lack of fiber and dehydration. Without water and fiber, the digestive waste products are not able to flow through the large intestine, causing constipation. This toxic waste remains in the intestine and is reabsorbed through the villi of the intestine into the blood stream where it can travel to all parts of the body causing countless problems,

Kidney damage can result from chronic dehydration.

Arthritis pain can be viewed as indication of water deficiency in the affected joint. Cartilage surfaces of bones in joints contain water. The lubricating property of water is utilized allowing the two opposing surfaces to freely glide over one another during joint movement. Water held in the cartilage of a joint is the lubricant that protects the contact surfaces of the joint. Without water, there is no protection from friction, and the pain that it causes. Actively growing blood cells in bone marrow take priority over the cartilage for available water. Pain is an indicator that the joint is not fully prepared to endure pressure because it is not fully hydrated.

Low back pain can indicate dehydration. 75% of the weight of the upper body is supported by water volume stored in the disc core. 25% is supported by fibrous material around the discs. Water is the lubricating agent that bears the force of the upper body weight. Without sufficient water, the weight of the body is not properly supported resulting in low back pain.

Neck pain has many possible causes including bad posture. The weight of the head forces fluid out of discs over time. Drinking water is necessary to replace lost water, and movement is essential for adequate fluid circulation.

Disease can be caused by lack of sufficient water. In prolonged dehydration, cells begin to shrink similar to a plum turning into a prune. Brain damage caused by dehydration has been hypothesized to be a causative factor in Alzheimer's disease. In prolonged dehydration, the brain cells begin to shrink, and many functions of brain cells begin to get lost, such as the transport system that delivers neurotransmitters to nerve endings.

Multiple Sclerosis symptoms have gone into remission with increased water intake. Allergies have been known to respond to an increase in water.

It is estimated that 12 million children suffer from asthma, and several thousand die each year. It is recognized that asthmatics have an increase in the histamine content of their lung tissue, and that it is this histamine which regulates the bronchial muscle contraction. Since one of the sites for water loss through evaporation is in the lungs, bronchial constriction produced by histamine means less water evaporation during the act of breathing – a simple natural maneuver to preserve the body water. Asthmatic children can be saved from the constant fear of suffocation by learning to recognize when they are thirsty for water!

Water is the solvent in the body. It regulates all functions including the activity of the solutes it dissolves and circulates. Proteins and enzymes function more efficiently in solutions of lower viscosity - less thickness or density. Water is a necessary to maintain proper balance.

Healthy looking skin needs water to constantly replace water lost by exposure to the environment. The single most important beauty tip you will ever learn is drink water! Your skin cannot look attractive if it is dehydrated. When toxins are trapped in the colon because there is not enough water or fiber in the diet, these toxins seek another method of escape – they will either remain in the body or leave directly through the skin!

Water is useful in weight loss. A glass of water 30 minutes before meals not only aids in digestion, but also acts as a healthful appetite suppressant. No weight loss medication is necessary.

Tea, coffee, carbonated water, alcoholic beverages, or juice cannot be substituted for plain water. They have central nervous system stimulants and act as a diuretic to the kidneys. Substituting other liquids for water will deprive the body of its full capacity for the formation of hydroelectric energy, among other things. Your body needs approximately eight glasses of water a day. The best times for water are a half hour before meals, and in between meals. Thirst should always be satisfied.

What kind of water should we drink? We are all cautious about tap water because we feel it is loaded with chlorine, and we have heard it can contain other undesirable elements. Did you know that Bottled Water is not much better? Water bottled and called 'Spring Water' is legally only required to be 10% spring water. The other 90% is tap water. Reverse osmosis robs water of its mineral contents, which are needed for optimal health.

What are the qualities of water that provide optimum health benefits? pH or 'potential

Hydrogen' measures if something is acid or alkaline. Nobel Prize winning Physicians have proven that cancer thrives in an acid environment. The water you drink should be alkaline. Bottled waters are acidic, and tap water is neutral. Ideally water should be antioxidant, which means that it does not contain the electrons that are considered 'free radicals'. Free radicals produce 'oxidation', the process by which things rot and rust, and also causes the aging processes such as facial wrinkling, etc. Water should be antioxidant, but most waters, especially bottled water are not.

Unfortunately, empty plastic water bottles are creating an ecological problem of gargantuan proportions, with serious consequences for future generations. The best water for your health and the well-being of the environment is filtered tap water. A good water filter is the best investment you can make. And be sure to drink the water!

Chapter 5 Rejuvenation and Detoxification

Rejuvenation means to make young or youthful again, give new vigor, restore, stimulate, and renew from stress by uplift and deep relaxation. Lifestyle is not just about what you eat, wear and do. It is also about how we treat ourselves and others. Rejuvenation, and Detoxification - the removal of harmful wastes, are part of that.

Massage Therapy has long been considered a popular form of relaxation and pampering. However, it also has serious medical benefits. This was scientifically proven at the University Miami School of Medicine, Touch Research Institute. Dr. Tiffany Field took blood, urine and saliva samples from patients before and after Massage Therapy. The results were a significant reduction in the stress related hormones present in the samples before massage, and significant increase in relaxation-related hormones after massage. This benefit has far-reaching medical consequences, because stress has been proven to be a significant factor in heart disease according to experts at Saint Francis Heart Hospital in Roslyn, New York. We all know that heart disease is one of the leading causes of death in the developed world.

In addition to heart disease, stress has been shown to be a contributing factor in other pathologies such as gastritis, colitis, irritable bowel syndrome, peptic ulcer, asthma, rheumatoid arthritis, migraine headaches, anxiety and depression. Stress has been proven to inhibit certain components of the immune system according to Hans Selig, a world authority on stress. Massage Therapy is also proven to enhance the immune system. Reducing the physiological effects of stress by Massage Therapy not only creates a feeling of relaxation and wellbeing, but also significantly contributes to longevity by eliminating one of the main causes of serious, life threatening illnesses.

Massage Therapy has been used to relieve muscle aches and pains for years. It works by eliminating the causes. Muscles produce energy through a chemical reaction ending with lactic acid as the final waste product. Lactic acid can build up in the muscle cells causing "knots" or "trigger points". This happens when the muscle cells are saturated with lactic acid, leaving no room for oxygen or nutrients. This anaerobic condition can be very painful. Massage Therapy gently applies pressure to these areas forcing the lactic acid and toxins to be flushed out of the body through the lymphatic system - the body's sewer system. The massage pressure creates a vacuum which, when released, draws fresh blood into the muscles. This fresh blood flow brings the necessary oxygen and nutrients to correct the painful condition. Massage also facilitates lymphatic drainage, because, unlike the body's circulatory system which pumps blood, the lymph is not pumped by the body. This can make a sedentary lifestyle unhealthy and toxic.

Massage Therapy also relaxes and strengthens muscles. This can be extremely beneficial in many diverse conditions. One of these is Temporomandibular Joint (TMJ). TMJ is named after the facial joint which connects the head and jaw. It is very common for this area to be injured in auto accidents when the victim is hit from the rear. This causes a whiplash effect to the head when snapped back and forth from the impact. The facial muscles that attach to the joint tighten significantly. Often this painful condition lasts for months or even years depending on the severity of the accident. Massage Therapy can hasten healing by helping the muscles begin to relax and go back to their original condition.

Herniated or "slipped discs" happen when the vertebral discs in the spine are no longer in a normal position. The muscles that help hold the spine in place, which in turn keep the discs in their normal position, surround the spine. Massage and exercise strengthen these back muscles, helping them to hold the spine and discs in the correct position. The stronger the back muscles, the less likely that an episode of disc problems will occur.

Massage Therapy relieves pain naturally, holistically. The manipulation of the body's soft tissue causes stimulation of nerves. When the body's nerves continue to be stimulated during the massage, the nerve receptors in the brain cannot process all the stimulations they are receiving. The massage acts as a pain block by over stimulating the nerve receptors in the brain. Often the effects last for hours, and sometimes even days. This eliminates the need for the use of pain medication that often has detrimental side effects.

There are many more specific conditions that can benefit from Massage Therapy. In addition to relieving pain and stress naturally, the general feeling of well-being resulting from Massage Therapy is indeed a life prolonging experience.

Swedish Massage is the most popular form of Massage Therapy. It dates back to the 1800's where it was first practiced by

Doctors in the hospitals of Stockholm, Sweden. It is based on the premise that improving the circulation removes impurities and toxins from the lymphatic system, flushes them out through the excretory system, while bringing fresh blood containing oxygen and nutrients to the cells. All strokes go in the direction of the heart to facilitate this process.

Swedish Massage stretches muscles and tendons, and removes lactic acid – the waste product of energy – from the muscles. Stress hormones are eliminated from the body and replaced with relaxation hormones, thus relieving stress. The stimulation of the nerves acts as a natural pain block.

Swedish Massage uses effleurage – long gliding soothing strokes, and petrissage – kneading, friction, vibrating, and tapotement. Oil facilitates the slide that is necessary on the skin to perform Swedish Massage. It is performed on a Massage table, and the patient is draped – the portion of the body not being worked on is covered.

Hot Stone Massage uses black basalt volcanic lava rocks, which absorb and retain heat. These are applied to the body in various places such as the palms of the hands, between the toes, points on the back, under the knees, etc. The stones are replaced as they cool and are also used in massage strokes. Heat facilitates healing by drawing blood to that particular area. The blood brings oxygen and nutrients to the affected area. The result is a maximum relaxing experience.

Aromatherapy is 6,000 years old. It was practiced in ancient Greece, Rome, and Egypt for health, healing and other uses. Essential oils are distilled from the leaves, flowers, roots, fruit, seeds, or bark of plants and trees. These essential oils contain the immune system of the plant, flower, or tree. Using essential oils boosts the human immune system to prevent disease transmission, and can treat a host of maladies from insomnia, bee stings to scars.

The essential oils are added to another oil – a "carrier oil" – and applied to the body.

They enter the body through the skin, which is permeable, and also through the olfactory system (smell) and go directly into the bloodstream. Essential oils are antiseptic, antiviral, anti-inflammatory, pain relieving, antidepressant. Each one has its own distinctive therapeutic psychological and physiological properties. During the plague in the Dark Ages in Europe, only the perfumers who worked daily with essential oils did not succumb to the plague. Aromatherapy is pleasant, preventative, and healing.

Reflexology is performed on the hands or feet. It is based on the scientific fact that the nerve endings in the hands and feet go to the brain and correspond with other nerves which end in other parts of the body. It is used to stimulate parts of the body which are not readily accessible such as internal organs. It has been used successfully to break up stones in the bladder that would have otherwise required surgery. In addition, it can be used to treat areas that are not able to be touched such as burned or injured parts of the body.

Facials can rejuvenate and enhance natural beauty by creating the optimal healthful environment for skin. Skin care involves deep pore cleansing and toning. Toners restore the skin to it correct, slightly acidic pH. This facilitates the functioning of the skin's acid mantle, which destroys harmful bacteria on the skin. Facials also include exfoliation which slough off the dead layer of skin to allow the fresh, new skin cells to emerge. Extractions remove sebum, built up dirt, grim, and blackheads in open pores. Facial massage provides relaxation, and a customized mask draws out impurities, hydrates, and has other beneficial properties based on the needs of the individual. The finale is the correct moisturizers and sun protection as well as recommendations for individual skin care regimes between facials.

Detoxification

Colonics are the ancient art of colon cleanse. The end products of digestion are toxic wastes which need to be eliminated from the body. Otherwise, they will be absorbed into the blood stream and poison the entire body. When an individual is constipated, the toxic waste remains in the colon and continues to ferment and putrefy.

Constipation is defined as having less than several bowel movements a day, or one bowel movement for each meal eaten. Chronic constipation affects a vast majority of people. This reduces their quality of life and health because the body is poisoning itself with toxic waste.

John Wayne's autopsy revealed that he had 40 pounds of fecal matter in his intestines at the time of his death. I am sure many people on a meat and dairy based, fiber free diet, have as much or more inside them every day! Maybe you have noticed all the big tummies!

Colonics are gentle, painless, non-invasive, and safe. Supplies are disposable; therefore, there can be no transmission of disease. The Client is draped modestly for the maximum privacy. The equipment used is U.S.F.D.A. approved. Only the purest water is used to cleanse the colon. The water is filtered through four filters and an ultra-violet light is used to kill bacteria for maximum purity.

Colonics rinse out the colon, or large intestine. The water does not go any further. The ileocecal valve is in between the small and large intestines. This one-way valve allows material to pass from the small intestine to the large intestine, but not back. Light massage alleviates discomfort and aids in elimination.

Maintaining colon health requires plenty of water and high fiber food. In addition, supplementing the diet with Probiotics assures the presence of "good" bacteria in the colon to maintain a proper balance with the "bad" bacteria. Enzyme supplements can aid in breaking down food in digestion. Herbal stool softeners are available for those times when a little natural help is needed between visits to the Colon Therapist.

Lymphatic Drainage is another form of detox. The lymphatic system is the body's sewer system. Cells perform many functions all resulting in waste products that are put into the lymphatic system. The circulatory system brings oxygen and nutrition rich blood to the cells and the lymphatic system removes waste. The difference is, unlike the circulatory system, which is pumped by the heart, the lymphatic system is not pumped. It is moved by gravity and exercise. People who lead sedentary lives have sluggish lymphatic systems. The toxic waste in the lymphatic system needs to be flushed out of the body for optimal health.

There are several versions of manual lymphatic drainage therapies. Besides the passive act of MLD, people can actively do simple exercises to facilitate lymphatic drainage. One of the most popular and effective methods for this is the trampoline. It is fun, healthful, and an easy way to flush the lymphatic system and detox the body.

Ear candling is a natural holistic method of gently and painlessly removing excess ear wax. It dates back to Biblical times when hollow reeds from swamp areas were utilized as candles. It has been passed down for many generations by the North and

South American natives, as well as the Egyptian, African, Oriental and European cultures.

Years of wax build up can cause hearing loss and deafness. This preventative therapy may render hearing aids unnecessary. In addition, it has been known to clear the sinuses. It is safe and effective. A specially made "candle" is used to create a vortex that draws out the excess wax. The Client is completely relaxed during the treatment. There are no side effects.

Infrared Sauna is recognized by Health Practitioners worldwide as perhaps the most effective method of removing both chemical and heavy metal toxins from the body. The skin is the largest organ in the body and the body's first line of defense. It is a permeable organ. Chemical contamination, household cleaners, paint fumes, and heavy metals can enter the body through the skin and exit the body through the skin. The infrared sauna has deep, penetrating heat which goes deep inside the body, releasing lipophilic (fat stored) toxins and heavy metals. As the body perspires, toxins and heavy metals are released.

A typical sauna cession will cause a brief, minor increase in body temperature, identical to the body's defense mechanism against bacteria, microbes, and consequent infection. This beneficial side effect triggers the production of white blood cells (leukocytes) by your bone marrow and killer T cells by your thymus. The result is immune system improvement.

A 20-minute session in an infrared sauna has the effect on the cardiovascular system similar to that from a six-mile run. The body's natural reaction to heat is to cool itself. It does this by diverting blood from the internal organs to the extremities and skin. This increases the heart rate, cardiac output and metabolic rate. Medical research indicates that use of infrared sauna therapy may be as effective a means of cardiovascular conditioning as regular exercise. This is especially important to individuals who are not physically capable of exercising. NASA concluded in the

1980's that infrared stimulation is the ideal way for astronauts to maintain cardiovascular conditioning during long space flights.

An optimal healthy lifestyle is achieved when the body is clean, relaxed, and refreshed.

Chapter 6 Exercise

Exercise is necessary for good health. It does not need to be torture! The most important thing is that you do it, even if it is once or twice a week. Find something you enjoy - that you can do with friends, in a class or group, or just by yourself. Find something that works for you! Here are two suggestions plus some inspiration from successful professional athletes who are living a plant-based lifestyle:

Yoga for Beginners and Intermediates uses gentle stretching and poses to improve posture by putting the body in alignment. It makes the body more powerful and increases the sense of well-being.

Brisk Walking is considered to be the best exercise for everyone and especially Cardiac patients. It is recommended by Doctors that people walk briskly for 30 minutes a day or an hour three times a week.

Athletic Inspiration. There are sound, scientific reasons that more and more athletes are becoming vegan to improve their performance. This will work for you too! You can improve your golf game, increase your stamina for tennis and swimming, and improve your overall enjoyment of life.

Here is "Why Athletes Are Racing To A Vegan Diet" according to Neal Barnard, M.D. Founder of Physicians Committee For Responsible Medicine (PCRM).

"Reduced Blood Viscosity and Improved Tissue Oxygenation. In the course of athletic activity, blood viscosity ("thickness") often increases, which causes a progressive loss of tissue oxygenation, potentially degrading athletic performance. Reduced viscosity, which can be achieved through plant-based diet, improves tissue oxygenation, reduces heart rate during exercise, and reduces dehydration. In a study of 48 individuals following vegan eating patterns, blood viscosity was significantly lower."

"Improved Blood Flow. Atherosclerosis reduces blood flow not only to the coronary arteries, but also to other parts of the body. By the age of 20, approximately 10 percent of the population in developed countries has advanced atherosclerotic lesions in the abdominal aorta, reducing blood flow and contributing to disc degeneration and lower back pain. Similarly, atherosclerosis can reduce blood flow to the legs, the brain, and other parts of the body. Plant based diets have been shown to reverse atherosclerosis, increasing blood flow to all parts of the body."

"Reduced Inflammation. Inflammation occurs not only in the artery walls contributing to atherosclerosis, but also in the joints and the soft tissues of the body. A 2017 review published in Public Health Nutrition found that vegan diets reduce inflammation. Researchers reviewed 18 prior studies, finding that individuals who followed a vegan diet for at least two years lowered their serum levels of C-reactive protein, a biomarker of inflammation, compared with those who did not follow a vegan diet."

Fruits, vegetables, grains and legumes are the ultimate power foods for more and more professional and amateur athletes. This includes Venus Williams, Ed Bauer. Bianca Taylor, Robert Cheeke, Mindy Colette, Seba Johnson, Austin Aires, Wilson Chandler, Lewis Hamilton, Holly Noll, Mike Zigomanis, Marcello Torres, and many, many more.

Here is what a few of them are saying:

"I became vegan when I was a skinny teenager. Over the next decade following a vegan diet, I gained 75 pounds and became a 2-time natural bodybuilding champion. Clearly, no meat was no problem for me." Robert Cheeke, Bodybuilder

"Vegan athletes are making an international impact on mainstream fitness. I feel great knowing that I'm not contributing to animal suffering. Now it's easier than ever to find delicious vegan options." Torre Washington, Bodybuilder

"I realized how absurd the notion of 'needing' meat in the diet was. I never looked back. I view it as a positive change and look forward to all of the new amazing, healthy, and delicious foods you can eat."
Mac Danzig, UFC Fighter

Vegan athletes are healthy, successful and they are incredibly courageous! The descendant of the most egregious human exploitation in history, Seba Johnson, a vegan Black athlete, is an inspiration not only in athletics but most especially in courage.

Seba Johnson is a vegan from birth and the first Black woman Olympic skier. She is also the youngest Alpine ski racer in Olympic history! She placed 28th out of 64 of the world's best in the Women's Giant Slalom at age 14 in the 1988 Winter Olympics in Calgary. She received death threats, hate mail and attempts to disrupt her safety then and through the following World Cup and World Alpine Ski Championship competitions. Skiing was considered a white man's sport.

Seba was born in St. Croix, US Virgin Islands. A vegan since birth, Seba learned about animal exploitation and attended protests with her mother. By her early teens, she held her own protests, once standing alone with a handmade sign outside of a zoo.

In the 1992 Winter Olympic Games in Albertville, France, Seba qualified for the 1994 Games in Lillehammer, Norway. She boycotted because Norway had resumed commercial hunting for whales. She was disqualified from a World Cup ski race for refusing to wear a ski suit with a patch of leather on it.

Seba stresses connecting moral and ethical regard for all humans and non-humans in order to completely eradicate all forms of oppression.

Even if you are not a professional, you can improve your stamina and endurance for golf, tennis, swimming, hiking, etc. You can be inspired by the courage and achievements of these and other vegan athletes.

Chapter 7 Preventing and Reversing Heart Disease

Heart disease is the leading cause of death for both men and women in the United States today. The single most important and extensive research study on this dilemma is the famous Framingham Heart Study. This study has been going on for generations and has studied both men and women, as well as their children and grandchildren. The results confirm the correlation between diet and heart disease.

According to the National Institute of Health, Office of Science Policy: The Framingham Heart Study: Laying the Foundation For Preventative Health Care:

"By the early 1920's, diseases of the heart consistently ranked as the #1 cause of death in the United States. Even the President was not immune to this emerging health concern: Franklin Delano Roosevelt died of hemorrhagic stroke in 1945 due to uncontrolled hypertension, raising awareness about the rising toll of cardiovascular disease. Driven by the need to understand this growing threat, the Framingham Heart Study ("Framingham") was started in 1948 by the U.S. Public Health Service and transferred shortly thereafter to the newly established National Heart Institute (now the National Heart, Lung, and Blood Institute (NHLBI) of the National Institutes of Health (NIH). One of the first long-term cohort studies of its kind, Framingham would become known as the crown jewel of epidemiology."

"The study has not only contributed enormously to our understanding of the natural history of cardiovascular disease and stroke, it also enabled us to identify their major casual risk factors. Framingham changed the way we study and approach chronic diseases in the medical and public health spheres. Thanks in large part to Framingham, we now go beyond treating disease once it occurs by emphasizing disease prevention and addressing modifiable risk factors. Framingham was an early pioneer in the use of epidemiology to study non-infectious diseases and gave rise to innovative methods that are being put to use in countless studies across the world. The overall impact of the Framingham Heart Study is vast, and the study continues to unveil new insights into human health to this day."

"The study, which is aimed to unravel the underlying causes of heart disease, started in 1948 with 5,209 participants in the town of Framingham, Massachusetts. Framingham is a longitudinal cohort study, a type of epidemiological study that follows a group of individuals over time to determine the natural history of certain diseases explore the behavior of those diseases and identify the factors that might explain their development. Part of the reason Framingham, Massachusetts was picked as the study site was because it was just big enough to provide a sufficient number of individuals for the study, while also small enough to be suited to the community approach of recruiting and effectively following participants over time.

Participants underwent physical examinations, gave blood samples for laboratory tests, and provided lifestyle and medical history information at regular intervals. Now a joint project of the NHLBI and Boston University, Framingham has expanded over the years, both in geographical and population scope. Today it includes many grandchildren and spouses in three generations of participants, as well as two cohorts of minority participants (the Framingham Omni Cohorts)."

"Now the concept of risk factors has paved the way for preventative approaches to disease. People can take control of their personal health risks through lifestyle modification and medical treatments."

"The Merck Manual's Centennial Edition listed Framingham as fourth among the 100 most significant advances in 20th-century medicine, behind only the development of antibiotics, mass immunization, and the discovery of vitamins."

Heart disease results when the coronary arteries which bring blood and oxygen to the heart start to narrow, pinching off blood flow, and threatening the viability of the heart. Arteries narrow due to the growth of small, raised areas, or little bumps, on the inside of the arteries which prevent normal blood flow. These bumps are called plaques. They are composed of cholesterol and fat, from meat, fish, and dairy. The body produces enough of its own cholesterol. Meat, fish, and dairy add extra unneeded cholesterol that ultimately restricts blood flow causing heart disease, strokes, and erectile dysfunction, among other things. These plaques start forming in young adulthood, sometimes even in childhood. Fortunately, a plant-based vegan diet has been proven to prevent and reverse heart disease.

Dean Ornish, M.D., a Harvard trained physician, published a study testing whether heart disease could be prevented and reversed without surgery or drugs. Using only a vegan diet, and lifestyle change, Dr. Ornish conducted an experiment. The control group received standard medical care. They were prescribed a diet centered on 'lean' meat, poultry, and fish, prescribed various medications, and advised not to smoke. The remaining patients were given no medication; and had only diet and lifestyle changes. They were asked to follow a low-fat vegan diet, take a brisk walk for either half hour every day, or for an hour three times a week, not to smoke, and to do stress management exercises.

After one year, all the patients had an angiogram. The control group following the traditional medical routine was worse. They still had chest pain, and still needed medication. Heart disease typically worsens over time. The patients in the experimental group were different. Their chest pain stopped within weeks, their cholesterol levels dropped dramatically, and their coronary arteries began to reopen. The results were published in "The Lancet" in 1990.

Caldwell Esselstyn, M.D., a Cleveland Clinic surgeon used the same vegan diet for severely ill heart patients. Some of the patients had been told they had less than a year to live. Those who stayed on the program had no cardiac events for the next 12 years. They had reversed their heart disease!

According to Caldwell B. Esselstyn, Jr., M.D, "Eleven years into my career as a surgeon, I became disillusioned with the treatment paradigm of U.S. medicine in cancer and heart disease. Little had changed in 100 years in the management of cancer, and in neither heart disease nor cancer was there a serious effort at prevention. I found the epidemiology of these diseases provocative, however: Three quarters of the humans on this planet had no heart disease, a fact strongly associated with diet."

The Framingham Heart Study has spent many decades tracking who gets heart attacks and who doesn't. Among its key findings is that the lower the cholesterol, the lower the risk of heart problems. While some authorities consider 200 mg/dl to be the boundary between desirable levels and high levels, the Framingham Study showed that a level lower than 200 is actually better.

In decades of research, not a single person in the Framingham Study with a cholesterol level below 150 had a heart attack.

Cholesterol is a raw material made in the cells of all sentient beings, including humans. It is used to make cell membranes and hormones, among other functions. Cholesterol is in a chicken breast or a salmon filet. Surprisingly, it is found mainly in the lean portions of meat.

Cholesterol in the foods you eat raises your cholesterol level. Animal products are the only significant source of cholesterol. Chicken has essentially the same cholesterol as beef. A single egg has 213 mg of cholesterol.

Saturated fats are sometimes called "bad fats". Their name comes from the fact that the fat molecule is completely covered with hydrogen atoms — that is, 'saturated' with them. If it is not covered with hydrogen atoms, it is called unsaturated. Saturated fats stimulate your own liver to make more cholesterol, which unsaturated fats do not.

Saturated fats are solid at room temperature, like cooled bacon grease. Vegetable oils are liquid at room temperature showing they are unsaturated fat. All fruit, vegetables, whole grains and beans are very low in fat overall, with absolutely no saturated fat or cholesterol.

The best way to lower your cholesterol and saturated fat is to avoid animal products. This is why Dr. Ornish's study used a vegan diet to reverse heart disease. Some Doctors still recommend 'chicken and fish' diets, which are not very effective. They only lower the amount of cholesterol in your blood by about 5 percent. A typical plant-based vegan diet lowers your cholesterol by about 20 percent.

From "Prevent and Reverse Heart Disease" by Caldwell B. Esselstyn, Jr., M.D.:

"Cholesterol is a white, waxy substance that is not found in plants – only in animals. It is an essential compound of the membrane that coats all our cells, and it is the basic ingredient of sex hormones. Our bodies need cholesterol, and they manufacture it on their own. We do not need to eat it. But we do, when we consume meat, poultry, fish, and other animal-based foods, such as dairy products and eggs. In doing so, we take non excess amounts of the substance. What's more, eating fat causes the body to manufacture excessive amounts of cholesterol, which explains why vegetarians who eat oil, butter, cheese, milk, ice cream, glazed donuts, and French pastry develop coronary disease despite their avoidance of meat."

"Heart disease develops in susceptible persons when blood cholesterol levels rise higher than 150 mg/dL. The converse is also true. A person who maintains blood cholesterol under 150 mg/dL for a lifetime will not develop coronary artery disease – even if he or she smokes, has a family history of coronary disease, suffers from hypertension, and is obese!"

"The New England Journal of Medicine reported on a study in which massive doses of cholesterol lowering drugs were used to reduce total cholesterol well below 150 mg/dL. Three out of four of the heart patients involved seemed to do very well under this regime. But it was not a complete success. Even with their cholesterol levels satisfactorily reduced, one out of every four of the patients in the study sustained a new cardiovascular event or died within two and a half years of starting this treatment...There had been no nutritional component to the study."

"The American Heart Association, the National Cholesterol Education Program, and the National Research Council – have decreed that serum cholesterol should be below 200 mg/dL. These same organizations suggest limiting fat consumption to no more than 30 percent of the calories consumed each day."

"But that level of fat consumption has never been shown to arrest or reverse coronary artery disease. Quite the contrary, research has shown that while cutting fat consumption to that level from even higher levels may help to slow the disease's progression, the disease, nonetheless, will progress."

"The truth is that the Medical profession knows better. We have known for a long time that one out of every four persons who have heart attacks has a blood cholesterol level between 180nand and 210 mg/dL. And we know that more than a third of those in the Framingham Heart Study who had heart disease showed cholesterol levels between 150 and 200 mg/dL. That means that millions of Americans who are doing the best they can to meet the standards set by national health officials are, in spite of their efforts, getting sick."

"Here's a clear, plain English translation of what our government and the national health agencies have done: they have chosen a "safe" cholesterol level for the public that virtually guarantees – if everyone actually met their stated goal – that every year more than 1.2 million Americans will suffer heart attacks and that millions more will watch the inevitable progression of their coronary artery disease."

"We are immersed in an environment of toxic food that is attractive, tasteful, reasonably priced, and heavily advertised. And there are powerful commercial interests that want no change in the American diet. Over the years, there have been a number of attempts to bring nutritional recommendations more into line with what the science actually knows. In every case, intensive lobbying by industry – the producers and purveyors of dairy products, meat, and poultry- has caused those who set the standards to pull their punches."

"There will always be special situations in which patients with unsustainable coronary artery disease will require some type of urgent bypass or intervention, but I am convinced that with improved nutrition, we can spare a growing majority of patients from these procedures. And I am pleased to see that quite a number of scholarly cardiologists are beginning to question the wholesale rush toward mechanical intervention in heart disease.'

"One of them is Dr. John Cooks of Stamford University, who readily acknowledges that angioplasty - while it can help to relieve angina – hardly ever saves lives and does nothing whatsoever to cure heart disease. He suggests, in fact, that about half of all angioplasties performed in the United States each year are simply unnecessary."

There are a plethora of healthy plant-based choices available for those who care about their health. Besides fruit, vegetables, legumes, and grains, there are now soy, almond and oat plant milks, vegan cheese, non-dairy frozen desserts, meat substitutes like meatless meatballs, chic'kn cutlets, crabless cakes, and many more. Holidays can be festive with cruelty free, and delicious tofurky. All this is in addition to the fruit, vegetables, grains and legumes on the plant-based vegan diet. There is no reason not to be well fed, happy and healthy!

Chapter 8: Understanding Diabetes

Worldwide about 200 million people have diabetes. Diabetes is diagnosed when someone has an unusually high level of glucose in their blood, experiences fatigue, is losing water rapidly, and has excessive thirst.

In order to understand diabetes, we need to start by understanding digestion and other basic functions of the human body. The digestive system uses enzymes to break down all the food – protein, carbohydrate, and fat – into smaller and smaller molecules. The end product of digestion is the smallest possible nutritional molecule – glucose.

Glucose is absorbed through the villi in the walls of the small intestine directly into the blood stream. The blood transports glucose and oxygen to all the cells of the body through smaller and smaller blood vessels to tiny blood vessels called capillaries.

Cells take in glucose and oxygen and dispose of carbon dioxide and the waste products of metabolism. When glucose is unable to enter the cells to nourish them, it must remain in the bloodstream. Eating sugar free foods will do nothing to change this. It will only put you at risk for the side effects of sugar substitutes.

Diabetes occurs when fat from meat, fish, and dairy fills the body's cells. This makes it impossible for glucose from digestion to enter and nourish the cells. If glucose cannot enter, and nourish fat filled cells, it stays in the blood stream. Glucose, a simple sugar, is removed from the blood by the kidneys and is excreted in urine causing the symptoms of diabetes.

Glucose is the energy source that powers everything: thoughts and movements. When cells are deprived of glucose for energy, fatigue is experienced. The glucose that cannot enter the cells remains in the bloodstream and becomes very concentrated. It takes copious amounts of water to excrete it, causing loss of fluids. This is often accompanied with weight loss indicating that the cells are starving. Type two diabetes is diagnosed when a Doctor takes a blood sample and finds an unusually high level of glucose.

There are two types of diabetes. Type one diabetes, also called childhood onset diabetes, and insulin dependent diabetes, is less common than type two diabetes. It is usually diagnosed in childhood and is invariably treated with insulin. Type one diabetes occurs when the immune system attacks and destroys the insulin producing cells in the pancreas. The immune system is not supposed to attack healthy body tissues. When it does, it is called autoimmune disease.

Genes are not solely responsible for this phenomenon. Identical twins have proven this. Often only one twin has type one diabetes while the other twin does not have diabetes. Studies have shown type one diabetes to be caused by a reaction to cow's milk in infants and young children. Unlike people with type two diabetes, people with type one diabetes always need insulin. However, they can use diet and lifestyle changes to keep doses to a minimum and reduce the risk of complications.

Insulin is produced in the pancreas. It is a hormone that is released into the blood stream and travels to various cells in the body. Like a key sliding into a lock, insulin attaches to a receptor on the cell's surface and allows glucose to enter. Diabetes occurs when insulin cannot get the cell to allow the glucose inside. This is called insulin resistance. There is nothing wrong with the insulin, the glucose, or the cell. The problem is in the cell's refusal to allow the glucose in. The reason for this is something is already in the cell occupying the space needed by the glucose. That something is fat. These traces of fat begin to accumulate many years before diabetes manifests.

Normally fat is burned up by mitochondria, little furnaces in the cells, to use as fuel for energy to power muscle cells. Studies prove that as fat in cells increases, the mitochondria avoid burning it, as if to save it for future use. Reducing fat in the diet has been proven to reduce fat in the cells.

Diabetic patients are asked to avoid sugar and starchy foods because they break down into sugar in the digestive tract. However, starchy foods are prevalent in the diet in Japan, China, Thailand, and other parts of Asia and Africa where diabetes is rare. When people from these cultures move to Europe or North America, where diabetes, heart disease and cancer are prevalent, they change to a meat and dairy based diet, and their incidence of diabetes skyrockets. As the traditional Japanese diet has changed to a meat and dairy based Western-style diet, the prevalence of diabetes explodes.

Hemoglobin is the pigment that gives color to red blood cells. Glucose enters red blood cells and sticks to hemoglobin. An A1c test shows how much glucose is stuck to the hemoglobin. Research shows that A1c values should be below 7% or better yet – 6.5%. The American Dietetic Association diet reduced Alc by 0.4%, but the plantbased vegan diet was three times more effective reducing Alc by an average of 1.2%. The vegan diet also reduced body weight and cholesterol. Studies show that a one point drop in Alc lowers the risk of eye and kidney complications by 37%.

In 1979, researchers at the University of Kentucky studied 20 men with type two diabetes, all of whom had been taking an average of 26 units of insulin daily. They were put on an experimental diet of vegetables, fruits, whole grains, and beans – in short – a vegan diet. The diet was high in fiber and carbohydrates, low in fat, and had no saturated fat or cholesterol that is present in meat and dairy. After 16 days on the program, more than half of the men were able to stop taking insulin entirely. For those remaining men, insulin doses were cut dramatically.

In 1992, a team of Canadian and Finish researchers published a study in the New England Journal of Medicine. They took blood samples from children newly diagnosed with type one diabetes. They found that each of the children had antibodies which were primed to attack cow's milk proteins, which are a biochemical match for a portion of human insulin producing cells. These antibodies are also capable of attacking the body's insulin producing cells.

In 1994, the American Academy of Pediatrics issued a report. Based on their studies, they determined that the risk of type one diabetes could be reduced if infants were not exposed to cow's milk. Dr. Benjamin Spock and Dr. Neil Barnard held a Press Conference to inform the public of these findings.

In 1999, research studies in Georgetown and George Washington University and in the National Institute of Health in 2003 came to the following conclusion: in type one diabetes, a plant-based vegan diet can get blood sugar under control, so medications are minimized. Guidelines are to avoid animal products (meat, dairy, eggs), keep vegetable oils to a minimum, and choose foods with a low glycemic index.

The glycemic index (GI) is a number that indicates how rapidly any given food releases sugar into the blood stream. A food with a high GI releases sugar into the bloodstream quickly. White bread has a high GI, and pumpernickel has a low GI. These results were published in Preventative Medicine (1999), the American Journal of Medicine (2005), and presentations on these findings were given at the American Diabetes Association Scientific meeting (2004), the American Diabetic Association, American Association of Diabetes Educators, and American Public Health Association (2005-6).

Researchers at the Imperial College School of Medicine in London studied individuals following a vegan diet compared to individuals who were the same age and body weight but ate a meat and dairy based diet. They found the intramyocellular lipid in the participants' calf muscles was 31% lower in the vegans than the omnivores.

Studies conducted at Georgetown University (1999), George Washington University (1999), studies funded by the National Institute of Health (2003), studies presented at the American Diabetes Association Scientific Meeting (2004), and published in the American Journal of Medicine (2005), with results presented at the American Diabetes Association, American Association of Diabetes Educators, and American Public Health Association (2005, 2006) determined the following: A vegan diet can protect your body from the disease process. In Type Two Diabetes, it can counteract insulin resistance. In Type One Diabetes, it can get blood sugar under control, so medications are minimized. These are the guidelines: (1) avoid animal products - meat, dairy, eggs.
(2) keep vegetable oils to a minimum. (3) favor foods with a low glycemic index.

The plant-based vegan diet is a preventative 'therapy' to avoid diabetes. It can also reverse Type Two Diabetes, and control

Type One Diabetes keeping medications to a minimum. The Vegan Diet is the only scientifically proven way to prevent, control, and reverse diabetes.

At the September 2009 United Nations Non-Governmental Organization (UN NGO) Conference on Disarmament in Mexico City I had the opportunity to have a conversation with Doctor Enrico Ruelas, Secretario, Consejo De Salubridad General, (Mexico's Department of Health). He was extremely concerned about Mexico's skyrocketing incidence of Diabetes. You do not have to go all the way to Asia to witness the results of transitioning from the traditional plantbased diet to the meat and dairy based diet.

It is right here in the Americas.

I informed Dr. Enrici of the correlation between the meat and dairy based diet and incidence of diabetes, and told him about the research Dr. Neal Barnard had done on diabetes in Washington D.C. Dr. Enrici told me in fluent English that he was grateful for all the help he could get. Unfortunately, Dr.

Barnard was out of the country at the time, so I could not ask him to contact Dr. Enrici. Instead, I purchased one of Dr. Barnard's books and mailed it to Dr. Enrici. I hope it helped. I hope this helps you to understand Diabetes and what you need to do to avoid it or reverse it.

Chapter 9 Combating Cancer

Your best defense against cancer is prevention. Cancer is currently the second leading cause of death in the developed world. Cancer starts deep within the cells of the body. In the cell, biological and chemical interactions occur constantly. Cells work hard to control the use of oxygen and various nutrients, communicate messages, create new substances, and build new cells. The trillions of cells in the body communicate, remove toxic substances, repair injured cells, and prevent cells with damaged genetic material from reproducing.

Cancer begins when something goes wrong in a cell. The genetic blueprint deep inside a cell's nucleus, DNA, can become damaged. An impaired cell multiplying out of control forms a tumor. This is the beginning of cancer. The tumor eventually invades healthy tissues and can spread to nearby tissues or enter the blood stream and metastasize - invade other organs or parts of the body.

Meat, chicken, fish, and dairy products are high in hormones and other carcinogens which speed the growth of abnormal cells. They contain no fiber which is necessary to eliminate excess hormones and toxins. The plant-based diet by comparison, is high in protein. It also contains antioxidants, and protective nutrients which help prevent cancer, and fiber which facilitates the removal of carcinogens and toxins.

Cancers most commonly occur where there is a continual turnover and division of cells. The most vulnerable areas are where old cells are continually sloughed off and new ones built: the skin, lungs, digestive tract; and in organs that secrete substances: the breast; and in organs of reproduction: the uterus, ovaries, and testes.

Carcinogens, cancer-causing chemicals found in certain foods, and tobacco, can damage the DNA in cells. Certain foods block carcinogens from entering cells and damaging DNA, or limit the damage that occurs. Even at later stages, out of control cell multiplication can be reduced or prevented. The mineral selenium in whole grains, and the brightly colored carotenoids found in vegetables and fruits have shown the ability to slow or stop cancer growth. Folic acid found in leafy greens, oranges, and legumes has also been proven to protect DNA.

Oxygen is fundamental to life. Yet some of this essential substance can become unstable and cause serious problems in the body. Chemical reactions can leave oxygen with too many electrons, making it a 'free radical'. Free radicals are highly reactive molecules looking for other molecules to react with. When they attack DNA inside cells, the cells can begin multiplying out of control, which is the beginning of cancer. Meats, especially ones that contain nitrates, feed free radicals. Antioxidants, which plant-based diets are rich in, keep free radicals in check, and protect DNA against carcinogens.

Researchers have studied people with cancer, and those seemingly protected from it. Studies have confirmed that genes are not the cause of cancer. Rather, eating habits, smoking, and drinking habits determine vulnerability to cancer. Adapting a plant-based vegan, rather than a meat and dairy based, diet can prevent cancer or alter its course once it has been diagnosed.

In hundreds of research studies, scientists have tracked how cancer rates differ among groups of people whose genetic backgrounds are similar, but their diets are different. A direct relationship between diet and cancer risk emerged. The people who eat more fruit, vegetables, and whole grains, and avoid meat, dairy and fatty foods have a much lower cancer risk. They take advantage of certain protective nutrients while avoiding risky foods. If cancer does develop, the dietary characteristics of the plant-based vegan diet tend to improve survival.

In Japan the traditional diet has plenty of rice and vegetables, and very little meat or dairy products. People who move from Japan to the United States trade their original diet for one heavy with meat and dairy. This causes their breast cancer rates to more than triple and prostate cancer to become almost five times as common. "Food, Nutrition and the Prevention of Cancer: A Global Perspective", was released by the World Cancer Research Fund and the American Institute of Cancer Research in 1977. In this landmark document, an international panel of experts reviewed more than 4,500 scientific studies and summarized the effects of diet on the most common cancer sites. They found the Leading Controllable Factors Associated with Cancer Risk:

Increased Risk: smoking, alcohol, meat and dairy consumption, animal fat / saturated fat, total fat, grilling and barbecuing (red meat, chicken, fish), salt and salting (as a preservative), obesity, inactivity, and exposure to hazardous materials.

Decreased Risk: fruit, vegetable and whole grain consumption, carotenoids (protective substances in orange, yellow, red and green vegetables and fruits), Vitamin C, fiber, and physical exercise.

Both the meat-based and plant-based diets supply plenty of protein. There is as much protein in a serving of lentils, beans, tofu, soy milk, veggie burger, or similar meat substitute, as there is in a similar size serving of beef, chicken, fish, milk, cheese, or eggs. The difference is in the fat, hormone, and fiber content.

The plant-based vegan diet has less fat, and no cholesterol or saturated fat. The meatbased diet is high in fat, cholesterol, saturated fat, and hormones which are linked to cancer, and contains no fiber, antioxidants, or vitamin C. Fiber plays an important role in helping the body eliminate excess hormones and toxic substances. Hormones, which speed the growth of cancer, are especially plentiful in milk, making it a serious health risk.

Studies have shown that calcium in milk does not seem to benefit bones. The 1997 Nurses' Study at Harvard proved that milk drinkers broke more bones than people who avoid dairy. Many vegetables are excellent sources of calcium without the side effects of hormone rich milk.

Your body's first anticancer defense is your immune system – specialized white blood cells that seek out and destroy cancer cells. Their strength depends on a number of things, including the food you eat, getting plenty of antioxidants, Vitamin C, fiber, carotenoids and omega fatty acids. The best source of omega fatty acids is ground flaxseed, flaxseed oils, canola oil, walnuts, and butternuts.

If you are undergoing cancer treatment, the right foods can support you in getting well. For many people, surgery or other treatments are essential. Use diet with other treatments, not instead of them. Do not return to old eating habits when the cancer crisis is over. Cancer cells can lurk in your system for years. The introduction of a plant-based vegan diet, exercise, and other lifestyle practices anytime from childhood to old age will help prevent cancer and be an invaluable aid in treating any cancer already in progress.

From "Meat and Cancer" by Michael Klaper, M.D.

"In October (2015), 22 scientists from 10 countries met at the International Agency for Research on Cancer (IARC) in Lyon, France to evaluate the carcinogenicity of the consumption of red meat and processed meat. "

"I was pleased, but not really surprised, when I read the IARC, the cancer agency of the World Health Organization (WHO), declared, after reviewing more than 1,100 epidemiological studies, that processed meats cause cancer and that red meat is a "probable" carcinogen, as well. "

"(1) The very act of cooking animal muscle oxidizes muscle proteins and forms heterocyclic hydrocarbons that are proven carcinogens.
(2)   A second surge of carcinogens is added to the stool mass when bacteria in the

gut digest the heme protein (from blood left in the animal's muscle) into more cancerprovoking chemicals.

(3)   Because animal muscle has no fiber in it, these carcinogen-carrying stool masses move more slowly through the colon, giving them an extra-long time to smear their cancer-causing chemicals on the wall of the colon.

(4)   The scientific links are not hard to see, nor is the predictable backlash and rationalizations that follow the WHO announcement. The message is clear: a diet based on seared, smoked and processed animal flesh is a deadly one. As a result, food choices should not be hard to make!"

From "The Vegan Starter Kit" by Neal Barnard, M.D.

"Cancer. Vegetables and fruits are rich in cancer-fighting micronutrients, including folate (think green leafy vegetables), vitamin C (citrus fruit), bet-carotene (orange vegetables), and Lycopene (tomatoes and watermelon), among others. Cruciferous vegetables (e.g. broccoli, Brussels sprouts, cabbage, kale, cauliflower, and their cousins) stimulate the liver to make enzymes that neutralize carcinogens that you may be exposed to."

"Fiber, which is abundant in foods from plants but absent from animal products, helps prevent colorectal cancer and also helps remove excess hormones that could otherwise contribute to cancer of the breast, prostate, and other hormone-sensitive organs."

"Myth: Soy Causes Cancer. Researchers have tracked the diets of thousands of women, observing that women consuming the most soy (soy milk, tofu, etc.) are less likely to develop breast cancer, compared with those having the least soy in their diets…It also turns out that, among women who have been previously treated for breast cancer, soy products reduce the risk of cancer recurrence."

"Cholesterol: Your body uses cholesterol in the same way a factory might use petroleum. Cholesterol is a raw material, and your body makes many things from it. Believe it or not, cholesterol is used to make certain hormones, including testosterone and estrogen. It is also inserted into the thin cell membranes that surround each cell in your body, and it acts as a kind of glue to hold the membranes together…your liver sends particles containing cholesterol into your bloodstream for your cells to use."

"For cancer researchers, Japan was a role model. Breast cancer was rare. And if Japanese women did get breast cancer, it was often less aggressive than cancer tended to be in American women, and they were more likely to survive. That all changed in the later decades of the twentieth century. Western eating habits began to invade Japan. Meaty business lunches became common place, and fast-food chains started to crop up, featuring hamburgers, chicken, and cheese. Between 1975 and 2000, breast cancer incidence doubled."

"The problem was not polluted water or radiation. The problem was food. A 2016 study found that Japanese women who had

Westernized their diets the most had an 83 percent higher breast cancer risk, compared with those who had stayed with more traditional eating habits. The same phenomenon has been shown in other countries: As meat and dairy product push plant-based foods off the plate, cancer rates rise.

"Cut the Fat" The value of cutting fat intake was put to the test in the Women's Intervention Nutrition Study (WINS). It included 2,437 women who had previously been treated for breast cancer. Some were asked to begin a low-fat diet. The others continued their usual diets. After five years, the risk of cancer recurrence was reduced by 24 percent in the low-fat group. To avoid excess fats, the first step is to skip animal products. This helps you avoid the worst actors, the saturated fats in dairy products and meat. In turn, your hormone levels adjust."

"Dairy hormones may affect your odds of surviving breast cancer. A California study of women diagnosed with breast cancer found that those consuming one or more servings of whole fat dairy products (e.g. butter and cheese) per day had a 49 percent increased risk of dying of their cancer over the twelve years of the study, compared with those who generally avoided these foods."

"Boost the Fiber. Plants have fiber. And fiber escorts unwanted hormones out of your body. The power of vegetables and fruits was put to the test in the Women's Healthy Eating and Living (WHEL) Study. The goal was not to prevent cancer, but rather to help women who already had been treated for breast cancer. The study included 3,109 women. Half were asked to have five fruit and vegetable servings each day. The other half were asked to have eight servings of fruits and vegetables, plus 16 ounces of vegetable juice each day."

"The researchers found that, indeed, the participants made significant diet changes. In the eight-a-day group, fiber intake rose from 22 to 29 grams per day, and fat intake fell from 28 percent of calories to 21 percent within the first year. Estrogen levels fell too. Serum estradiol concentrations fell as well. That proves the point that changing your diet can indeed change your hormones. It really does work."

"Soy Cuts cancer Risk. Soybeans contain isoflavones, which have a chemical structure that is vaguely similar to testosterone or estrogen and, in test tube experiments, have been shown to attach to estrogen receptors. At first, that led some to speculate that soy products might cause cancer. However, scientific studies have shown just the opposite. In numerous studies, women who consume the most soy products have been shown to have about 30m percent lower risk of developing breast cancer, compared with their soy-avoiding friends."

"A surprising body of evidence has linked dairy products with prostate cancer." Two large Harvard studies investigated the connection and found that milk-drinking men are much more likely to develop prostate cancer, compared with men who generally steer clear of dairy products. The first of these, called the Physicians' Health

Study, included 20,885 men and found that those who had at least two and a half dairy servings per day had a 34 percent increased risk of developing prostate cancer. The second, called the Health Professionals Follow-up Study, included 47,781 men and found that men drinking more than two milk servings per day were 60 percent more likely to develop prostate cancer."

"In 2016, researchers looked at the full body of evidence to date. Combining the results of eleven different studies, they found that men consuming the most milk products has a 43 percent higher risk of dying from prostate cancer, compared with men who generally avoided dairy products."

"Testicular cancer is the most common cancer in men between the ages of twenty and forty-five. Dairy products, especially cheese, have been identified as suspects in several studies. A 2003 study showed that men consuming the most cheese had 87 percent higher risk of developing testicular cancer, compared with men who ate little or no cheese. Needless to say dairy products contain estrogen traces that are more concentrated as milk is turned into cheese. Processed meats (eg. sausage, bacon, turkey bacon, ham, and hot dogs) are also linked to higher risk."

"Cancer and Vegan Diet" by William Harris, M.D.

"I performed multiple regression analysis on breast cancer incidence. The highest correlation with breast cancer incidence was from animal source calories as compared to plant source calories. The saturated fat in meat and milk products increases the risk of breast cancer."

By now, it must be apparent that your best defense against cancer, and many other illnesses is the plant-based vegan lifestyle. In addition to being the best for your health, it also has the added benefit of being the best for the planet, for other people who share this planet with us, and for everyone of all species.

Chapter 10 Hormones and Autoimmune Disease

Many human illnesses are thought to be the result of hormones or lack of hormones, are unavoidable, or that the human body is mysteriously attacking itself. Although these issues may seem unrelated, they have one thing in common: vegans don't get them. Need I say more? In case you are not convinced, here is what the experts say:

Neal Barnard, M.D. "Your Body In Balance The New Science of Food, Hormones, and Health"

"When Menopause Became A Diagnosis"

"In North America, many people no longer think of menopause as a natural stage of life.

It has become a diagnosis, due in large part to the pharmaceutical industry.

"In 1941. Premarin was first marketed in Canada for the treatment of hot flashes. It was introduced in the United States the following year. Despite the fact that the drug comes from horse urine, American women were lured to it by promises of remaining young, vibrant, sexual, and wrinkle-free."

"Before long, however serious problems emerged. Women taking Premarin had strokes, dangerous blood clots, and dementia more often than the women taking the placebo. Women taking Prempro had all those risks too, plus a higher risk of breast cancer and heart attacks…"

"Overall, women taking the hormone combination ended up with a 29 percent higher risk of coronary heart disease, a 26 percent higher risk of invasive breast cancer, a 41 percent higher risk of stroke, and a doubling of their risk of blood clots in the lungs."

"Using Premarin alone, there is an increased risk of endometrial cancer (except for women who have had a hysterectomy), stroke, dangerous blood clots, and dementia. Using Prempro, there is an increased risk of stroke, heart attacks, breast cancer, blood clots, (including potentially fatal blood clots in the lungs, called pulmonary embolism), and dementia. Sales dropped and as women said no, breast cancer rates dropped too."

It is a scientific fact that hormone levels in women are elevated during the reproductive years. Hormone ladened meat and dairy add to this abundance of hormones. Vegan women have elevated levels of hormones, but only their own hormones, not those of others. As the reproductive years end, hormone levels in women drop. Vegan women seem to experience a much gentler menopause.

Vegan women do not experience extreme symptoms during menopause that non-vegan women experience and can get relief from any uncomfortableness by eating a little soy.

This can be as simple and easy as having soy 'faux cream cheese' on a bagel for breakfast instead of oatmeal. Wow! That was difficult! The phytoestrogen in soy relieves symptoms and is okay for men and boys to eat without any feminine side effects.

Neal Barnard, M.D. "Your Body In Balance

The New Science of Food, Hormones, and Health"

"A Healthy Thyroid"

"The thyroid gland sits at the base of your neck, shaped vaguely like a butterfly. Despite its size, it has a big job. It oversees your body's use of energy. That is to say, it maintains your body temperature and keeps your heart, brain, and muscles working right.

"That's your thyroid. It gives you the energy you need – or at least it tries. It works by sending thyroid hormones into your bloodstream, reaching every organ in the body. If you are running low on thyroid hormones, you'll feel sluggish and cold. If your thyroid overproduces its hormones, you may feel warm and have a rapid pulse and other symptoms of being revved up. Thyroid problems are very common."

"Hypothyroidism"

"An underactive thyroid can lead to fatigue, sensitivity to cold, dry skin, constipation, and weight gain. If things worsen, you might notice puffiness in your face, hoarseness, weakness, joint and muscle aches, hair loss, depressed mood, and noticeable gaps in your memory. Your cholesterol levels can rise and menstrual periods can become heavy and irregular. Your thyroid can enlarge – which Doctors call a goiter – as your thyroid struggles to improve its hormone output."

"Hyperthyroidism"

"If your thyroid produces too much thyroid hormone, the effects are more or less the opposite of hypothyroidism. Instead of feeling cold, an overactive thyroid can make you feel too warm. Instead of gaining weight, you are loosing weight without intending to. You may also experience a rapid or irregular heartbeat, a tremor in your hands, nervousness, irritability, weakness, and difficulty sleeping. Your hair can become fine and brittle, and your skin can become thinner. Women may find their periods are lighter or less frequent, and bowel movements can become more frequent."

"A Menu For A Healthy Thyroid"

"Iodine" found in iodized salt and seaweed."

"Avoid animal products.   People who avoid meat, dairy products, and eggs have been shown in research studies to have the lowest risk of hypo- or hyperthyroidism."
Autoimmune Disease

Autoimmune disease occurs when the body attacks itself. This is what happens in Multiple Sclerosis (MS), rheumatoid arthritis, lupus, Type 1 Diabetes, rheumatic heart disease. This is thought to be caused by the body's reaction to milk.

John McDougall, M.D. "The McDougall Program"

"Multiple Sclerosis is common in Canada, the United States, Northern Europe; it is rare in Japan, elsewhere in Asia and in Africa. When people migrate from a country of low incidence of multiple sclerosis to a country of high incidence, their chance of getting this disease increases as they learn new ways to eat and live."

Alzheimers

Aloysius Alzheimer. born on June 14, 1864 in Markbreit, Germany, was a German psychiatrist and neuropathologist and colleague of Emil Kraepelin. Alzheimer is credited with identifying the first published case of "presenile dementia", which Kraepelin would later identify as Alzheimer's disease.

According to Dr. Neal Barnard, "In 2003, Chicago researchers reported a stunning finding: People who generally avoided "bad" fats dramatically reduced their risk of developing Alzheimer's disease. In this case, "bad" fats mean two things: the saturated fat (solid fat) found in dairy products and meat and the trans fats (partially hydronated oils) found in snack foods."

"Vitamin E-rich foods reduce Alzheimer's risk. That means almonds, walnuts, sunflower seeds, pecans, pine nuts, pistachios, sesame seeds, and flaxseed. Go easy, because these are fatty, high calorie foods. Just one handful of nuts or seeds a day is plenty."

Alzheimer's disease has also been alleged to be caused by chronic dehydration of the brain with the resulting shriveled brain cells no longer being able to function. This should be an inspiration to all to adopt a plant-based diet and drink plenty of water!

Allergies

Allergies can be relieved by eliminating meat and dairy from the diet. Other culprits are artificial sweeteners, soda, chemical additives and preservatives. Individuals who have celiac are allergic to the protein in wheat called gluten. Only a very few people have this particular allergy. Drinking plenty of water can help in combating allergies.

Arthritis

Pain from arthritis is linked to dairy. Eliminating all dairy, including not only milk, but also eggs, and yogurt will eliminate the pain. It will take approximately one month to get results. After that, the pain will be gone until the next time you eat dairy. Then in a few days of abstaining from dairy, the pain will be gone again. Try it! I know people it has worked for!

Chapter 11 Zoonotic Disease

Zoonotic diseases, the cause of most epidemics and pandemics, are caused by human – animal interaction. Globally, many of the most serious infectious diseases are zoonotic, causing an estimated 3 million human deaths per year before the current Covid-19 pandemic. A zoonotic disease is caused by a pathogen that jumps, or "spills over", from animals to humans. Infections are then transmitted directly among humans. Pathogens include prions, viruses, bacteria, protozoa, parasites, and fungi. Zoonotic disease may be vector born, foodborne, or waterborne.

Emerging diseases are almost invariably zoonotic. An estimated 60% of all viruses that infect humans came from animals, and 75% of all new infectious diseases in the past decade are zoonotic. Examples include Covid-19, Human Immunodeficiency Virus (HIV), Ebola virus, SARS, MERS, Swine Flu, and Avian Flu, among many, many others. Zoonoses have caused the deadliest pandemics in history: Black Death, Spanish

Flu, HIV, and now Covid-19. The global rate of zoonotic disease is increasing. Without understanding the creation and spread of zoonoses, and rectifying these issues, it is impossible to prevent the next pandemic.

COVID-19 originated from an animal sold in a live animal market either to be eaten or used for Chinese medicine. Scientific evidence indicates that the virus originated from a bat coronavirus, then transferred to an intermediate host, either a domestic or wild animal, either in the wild, or kept in captivity. It ultimately evolved into SARSCoV-2, the coronavirus responsible for COVID-19, spread to an animal in a live animal market, and then to humans. Covid19 is the direct result of the unjust systematic abuse and exploitation of other species by the human species. This cause is almost never mentioned and is never addressed in the effort to overcome it.

HIV/AIDS, also from zoonotic origins, is one of the most serious public health threats of the 21st century. More than 33 million people worldwide are infected with HIV and more than 25 million people have died from the disease. HIV/AIDS originated when an established SIV switched from primates to humans through exposure to blood or other secretions of infected primates. This occurred through the hunting and butchering of innocent wild animals to be used as 'bush meat'. Bites and other injuries caused by primates kept as pet animals can cause a viral transmission according to 'Future Medicine'.

Ebola virus disease (EVD), also from zoonotic origins, is a deadly disease with outbreaks that occur primarily on the African continent. It is caused by an infection with a group of viruses within the genus Ebolavirus: according to the Center for Disease Control and Prevention (CDC).

Avian (Bird) Flu (H5N1) in 1997, and Swine (Pig) Flu (H1N1) in 2009 emerged from agricultural facilities - factory farms - with horrific conditions. H5N1 has an estimated mortality rate of 60 percent and could easily mutate and become more lethal.

H1N1 is believed to have originated in pigs in North Carolina resulting in more than 200,000 infections and 18,000 human deaths, including 250 children. Innocent, exploited pigs and birds suffered much higher casualties! According to the World Health Organization (Who), the 1997 outbreak of H5N1 resulted in the death of an estimated 1.5 million chickens and other birds. The infamous 'Great Influenza' of 1918 – 19, also zoonotic, sickened one third of the world's population and resulted in the death of over 50 million people. The horrific exploitation of domestic and wild birds was the cause.

Modern food production involves billions of high-risk interactions between humans and animals. Innocent, incarcerated animals in the food system are relentlessly stressed, confined, forced to share space with dead or diseased animals, share bodily fluids and airborne pathogens, expel waste on each other, all while being fed a steady supply of antibiotics. The physiological stress that animals endure weakens their immune systems making them much more likely to become vectors of disease. The system invites zoonotic disaster.

Factory farms are epicenters of disease for humans as well as the billions of unfortunate animals involuntarily incarcerated there.

Thousands of genetically similar animals are packed together in unsanitary, overcrowded spaces. They are vulnerable to disease and stress placed on their immune systems by these horrific conditions. Factory farms are ideal environments for viruses and other pathogens to circulate, mutate and 'spill over' to human exploiters. United Nations Food and Agriculture Organization (FAO) maintains that farmed animals are the weakest link in our global health.

An estimated 99% of the ten billion land animals murdered for food every year in the US alone are imprisoned in factory farms, and murdered with impunity. Innocent animals in factory farms or live markets are severely stressed, cannot engage in natural behaviors, experience frustration, and maladaptive behaviors such as injuring or murdering one another out of survival instinct. Pigs can drop dead from the stress of being confined. All these conditions make animals (amplifier hosts) more susceptible to pathogens, which then get passed on to their human abusers (bridge population), and the human population in general through zoonotic pandemics.

Live Markets, or 'wet markets', offer the sale and on-site slaughter of a multitude of innocent animals, including rare and wild animals. This often includes endangered or threatened wild animals, and other animals who would never come into contact with one another in the wild. These markets exist all over the world. Covid-19 is believed to have started in one in Wuhan, China. Customers purchase these animals for both consumption and traditional Chinese medicine.

Eighty percent of the antibiotics produced worldwide are fed to unjustly incarcerated animals raised to be consumed by humans. As a result, people suffer antibiotic resistant infections, with a high percentage resulting in mortality. This is in addition to the unparalleled suffering being caused to the sentient beings forced to endure this insanity. It is now well established that abuse of antibiotics fosters new antibiotic resistant diseases for which people will eventually have no defense. According to the World Health Organization (WHO) 'We are headed for a post-antibiotic era, in which common infections and minor injuries can once again kill.'

Zoonotic pandemics are inevitable given the increasing incursion of human beings into wildlife habitat. 75% of earth's land areas have already been heavily transformed by human activity. Species are presently going extinct at approximately 1,000 times the natural rate. Habitat destruction, biodiversity loss, and humanity's attendant encroachment on wildlands add to the risk of zoonotic disease. Scientists agree that habitat loss is positively correlated with increased zoonotic disease. This is because high biodiversity reduces the risk of zoonotic disease by the 'Dilution Effect'. High biodiversity actually protects human health by reducing the risk of zoonotic disease.

The widespread routine use of manure as fertilizer, and irrigation with contaminated water is a real concern. Salmonella and E. coli can spread to vegetables and contaminate them. A sustainable alternative to manure is veganic agriculture which uses no animal inputs. Instead, it uses 'green manure' - plowed under nitrogen rich cover crops. Pathogen runoff from intense animal imprisonment can permeate human water supplies leading to bacterial contamination of rivers and streams impacting both humans and wildlife. These pathogens include fecal coliforms, Streptococcus, Campylobacter, Giardia, Cryptosporidium, E. coli, as well as viruses, all resulting from the unjust exploitation of other species.

Animal exploitation comes with the accompanying skyrocketing health care costs. The resulting economic burden will be unsustainable in the developing nations.

The current human / animal relationship is unjust and unsustainable. This troubled relationship with animals keeps humanity at risk of zoonotic outbreaks, directly resulting from exploitation of animals and the environment we share with them. It is impossible to humanely and safely confine and exploit animals. This has not worked. The United Nations recommendation of stricter regulations of live markets, the UN Universal Declaration of Animal Welfare, and global investigations have not been effective in solving the problem. Neither have any local or national laws or ordinances.

Currently in the world today, the non-human population outnumbers human population by literally billions. This is not because of wild animal populations. Species extinction and habitat destruction are causing these individuals to quickly disappear. This gigantic difference in population is the individuals raised in the horrific conditions that breed disease and suffering – animals raised and murdered for human food. Under these circumstances, pathogens appear which threaten the lives, health, and incomes of the worldwide human population who eat these individuals, and their eggs, and drink their milk.

Epidemics are the direct result of speciesism – the abuse and exploitation of other species for the benefit of the human species.

The World Health Organization (WHO) defined the outbreak of COVID-19 as a public health emergency of international concern. Another concern is the H5N1 virus infection which has proven fatal for chickens (and sometimes other poultry) as well as for human beings. With poultry and eggs now the major source of meat protein worldwide, this fact has implications for food supply and international trade. It also raises the possibility that human beings and chickens can be cross-infected, and in the absence of tight biosecurity, the virus potentially spreading in pandemic mode.

Researchers have found 13 zoonoses, animal to human diseases, were responsible for 2.2 million human deaths every year even before the Covid-19 pandemic. These are:

zoonotic gastrointestinal disease; leptospirosis; cysticercosis; zoonotic tuberculosis (TB); rabies; leishmaniasis; brucellosis; echinococcosis; toxoplasmosis; Q fever; zoonotic trypanosomiasis; hepatitis E; and anthrax. Other pandemic diseases resulting from species transmission include: Coronaviruses - the large family of viruses that can cause diseases ranging from the common cold to Severe Acute Respiratory Syndrome (SARS) and Middle East Respiratory Syndrome (MERS), a viral respiratory disease caused by a novel coronavirus (MERS-CoV) first identified in Saudi Arabia in 2012, as well as Covid-19.

Although zoonotic pandemics affect the entire world, Africa will suffer most from Covid-19. Currently Africans are at great risk of dying from measles and malaria. The disruptive infectious potential of the deadly Covid-19 pandemic will undermine efforts to control malaria. As of March 2020, malaria-endemic regions in Africa reported a few Covid-19 cases in Nigeria, Senegal, and the Democratic Republic of the Congo. There are additional complications for malaria-endemic regions from a novel infectious disease outbreak. The 2014–16 outbreak of Ebola virus disease in West African malaria-endemic countries, including Guinea, Liberia, and Sierra Leone, led to a public health emergency and disrupted malaria control efforts. More alarmingly, it was estimated that there were about 7,000 additional malaria associated deaths among children younger than 5 years in Guinea, Liberia, and Sierra Leone due to the Ebola outbreak. It is even more difficult for malaria endemic regions when faced with the threat of a novel infectious disease outbreak.

Many livestock infected with zoonoses are in low-income nations. A large percentage show signs of brucellosis, trypanosomiasis, zoonotic tuberculosis, cysticercosis, leptospirosis, leishmaniasis, echinococcosis, toxoplasmosis, hepatitis E, and anthrax, as well as signs of current or past infection with bacterial food-borne diseases that cause food contamination. Worldwide 12 percent of animals have recent or current infections with brucellosis, 10 percent of livestock in Africa are infected with trypanosomiasis, 7 percent of livestock are currently infected with TB, 17 percent of smallholder pigs show signs of current infection with cysticercosis, 26 percent of livestock show signs of current or past infection with leptospirosis, and 25 percent of livestock show signs of current or past infection with Q fever.

According to the United Nations World Health Organization (WHO) the greatest threat to international health security is outbreaks of epidemic diseases. Factors fueling these outbreaks are the way food is produced and traded, and the way antibiotics are used and misused. Antibiotics used on humans to treat diseases of a zoonotic nature can result in antibiotic resistance. According to the United States Center for Disease Control, there are an estimated 2 million drug-resistant infections that occur in the United States alone each year causing 23,000 human deaths. The billions of unjustly incarcerated and ultimately executed individuals raised for food are routinely given antibiotics in their food and water to stimulate growth, while simultaneously enabling them to survive in the disease-ridden horrific conditions on factory farms.

Accompanying the mortality and morbidity of pandemic incidents is the devastating economic loss to individuals and businesses across the planet. With people staying home to avoid contracting the disease, many businesses are experiencing loss, and individuals who do not go to work experience loss of pay. Investors feel the loss in the stock markets due to declining productivity. Just as in the worldwide phenomenon of hoarding toilet paper, some individuals are motivated to have much while leaving nothing for others.

Animal exploitation comes with the accompanying skyrocketing human health care costs. The resulting economic burden will be unsustainable in the developing nations. One species dominating all other species cannot exist without precipitating catastrophic events.

Corona virus 2019 (Covid-19), as well as Severe Acute Respiratory Syndrome (SARS), Middle East Respiratory Syndrome (MERS), "Swine Flu", avian influenza viruses (H5N1, H9N2, and H6N1 from poultry) and other epidemics are the result of Speciesism, supremacy of one species (human) over all others. According to researchers, most human infections with zoonoses come from livestock, including pigs, chickens, cattle, goats, sheep and camels. Zoonoses from the livestock sector, animals raised for human food, cause the most human deaths.

There is no way to humanely, safely confine and exploit animals. This has not worked. The United Nations recommendation of stricter regulations of live markets, the UN Universal Declaration of Animal Welfare, global investigations, local and national laws and regulations have not been effective in solving the problem. What is needed is a radical, comprehensive approach. Vegan

International, a United Nations Economic and Social Council (ECOSOC) NonGovernmental Organization (NGO), is advocating a United Nations Convention Against Speciesism to resolve this issue.

Exploited animals are innocent individuals who suffer the loss of their children, violation of their bodies, experience fear and pain, are tortured and murdered with impunity, and have absolutely no recourse. Their exploitation is an unjust war on the defenseless. Their lives are calling out for justice, and we are experiencing a portion of that justice now. The full force of justice – an even worse pandemic, which can happen - will be even more devastating than Covid19! It is time to take positive action!

The human species will not experience peace or real safety while continuing to exploit and degrade other species. Everyone deserves justice, and the United Nations' "place at the table" regardless of species. The United Nations motto, "No one left behind", should apply to everyone on planet

Earth, not just to one species. There needs to be a radical, comprehensive approach.

Vegan International is advocating a United Nations Convention Against Speciesism to follow the UN Conventions against Genocide, Torture, Elimination of Discrimination Against Women, and Rights of the Child. Like President Abraham Lincoln's Emancipation Proclamation, it is a necessary step toward equality, justice, and safety for all.

Chapter 12 World Response To Zoonotic Disease

This is from a Vegan International Newsletter:

"The United Nations General Assembly 31ˢᵗ Special Session – In Response to the Coronavirus Disease Covid-19 Pandemic discussed a plethora of ideas. These included the disproportionate adverse effect on women and girls being victimized by violence from frustrated men. There are currently 2.5 million more child marriages, and a high rate of death from childbirth in girls 15 to 19 years old. Eleven million girls are at risk of not going back to school after the pandemic. Violence against children 2 to 17 years old is up to one billion. Hundreds of millions of children have been out of school. Refugees, displaced persons, migrant workers, and the countries that host them, are particularly vulnerable. The poorest countries are the most impacted. Worldwide there were eight million people in hunger increasing to135 million in the last four years. This has now spiked to 270 million people starving during the Covid pandemic. Efforts to provide clean water, nutrition and health care in developing nations have been seriously affected. The pandemic has exacerbated efforts to combat other lethal diseases including malaria and measles. The poorest countries are the most impacted. The crisis is especially difficult in Small Island Developing States (SIDS) whose economies depend primarily on tourism. 235 million people may not survive 2021."

"Vaccines are currently available, but there is not enough money or vaccines worldwide. There are no vaccine distribution mechanisms in developing nations. UNICEF, WHO, and GAVI will attempt to finance and distribute vaccines in remote areas. The maxim: 'No one is safe until everyone is safe', needs to be embraced."

"Only once during the Special Session was the actual cause of the pandemic referred to: 'Wet markets should be closed.' Only one speaker, Pavan Sukhdev, from United

Nations Environmental Program (UNEP), referred to the inability to live in harmony with nature, and habitat destruction, in relation to pandemic disease. Ten percent of the Earth's forests have been lost, causing closer interaction between humans and other species. Habitat destruction and species extinction makes transmission of disease more likely to happen. High biodiversity reduces the risk of zoonotic disease by the 'Dilution Effect', protecting human health. Mr. Sukhdev said further that chemical farming is destroying soil, and referred to natural farming (also known as Veganic Agriculture) which produces higher yields at lower costs, without risk of the disease producing contaminants Escherichia coli, Salmonella, and others from animal exploitation."

"THERE WAS NO MENTION OF THE CAUSE OF THE CURRENT GLOBAL HEALTH AND ECONOMIC CRISIS: EXPLOITATION OF VOICELESS, RIGHTLESS SPECIES BY THE HUMAN SPECIES."

"The United Nations Summit on Biodiversity recently stressed urgent action on biodiversity for sustainable development. The summit provided a "Voices For Nature" platform, and highlighted the goal of "Living in Harmony with Nature". Biodiversity loss and ecosystem degradation are currently among the top threats facing humanity - jeopardizing food security, water supplies, weakening human ability to fight diseases, causing extreme weather events, and exacerbating geopolitical tensions and conflicts. ACCORDING TO THE SUMMIT, THE EMERGENCE OF DEADLY ZOONOTIC DISEASES SUCH AS HIV/AIDS, EBOLA, AND COVID 19 ARE A CONSEQUENCE OF HUMAN IMBALANCE WITH NATURE. SPECIFICALLY, THE EXPLOITAITON OF OTHER SPECIES BY HUMANS."

"The fundamental issue is very simple. It is Speciesism – the exploitation by one species - humans, of all other species. The results of speciesism are destroying the planet: climate change, pandemics, human mortality and morbidity, species extinction, loss of biodiversity, pollution of air, water, and land, and misuse of scarce resources, among others. MOST IMPORTANTLY, THIS IS A JUSTICE ISSUE AND A LEGAL ISSUE: THE LACK OF RIGHTS OF EXPLOITED, VOICELESS INDIVIDUALS."

"Currently there are enforceable non-human rights in the Constitution of Ecuador. 'Rights for Nature' does not treat nature as property under the law, it acknowledges that nature in all its life forms has the right to exist, persist, maintain and regenerate its vital cycles, and that people have the legal authority to enforce these rights on behalf of ecosystems. This shining example needs to include all species, be accepted, and implemented everywhere."

Chapter 13 United Nations World Health Organization Weighs In

United Nations World Health Organization (WHO) is the directing and coordinating authority for health within the United Nations system. It is responsible for providing leadership on global health matters, shaping the health research agenda, setting norms and standards, articulating evidence-based policy options, providing technical support to countries and monitoring and assessing health trends.

According to the United Nations World Health Organization, one of the greatest threats to international health security arises from outbreaks of emerging and epidemicprone diseases. One of the factors fueling these outbreaks is the way food is produced and traded, and the way antibiotics are used and misused.

According to WHO Director General Margaret Chan, "A post-antibiotic era means an end to modern medicine as we know it. Things as common as strep throat or child's scratched knee could once again kill."

According to the U.S. Center for Disease Control, there are an estimated 2 million drug-resistant infections that occur each year with a staggering 23,000 deaths. Animals raised for food are routinely given antibiotics in their feed and water. This is done to stimulate growth while simultaneously enabling stressed animals to survive in the disease- ridden conditions on factory farms.

The United Nations motto: 'No one is safe until everyone is safe" could not be truer. Unfortunately, they seem to have missed the point that 'everyone' needs to include everyone. There are no provisions anywhere for the safety of the most vulnerable - the exploited and eaten individuals of other species, whose endless suffering has now been passed on in the form of the Covid-19 pandemic.

Chapter 14 Starvation of the Vulnerable Linked to Diet of the Affluent

Of the Earth's nearly 7 billion human beings, roughly 1 billion people are malnourished, 20 million people, including 6 million children, die from malnutrition annually as a direct result of the affluent's meat and dairy based diet. Worldwide, developing nations sell their grain to the developed nations often while they and their own children are starving.

The developed nations fed this grain to their livestock - innocent, unjustly incarcerated individuals, so that consumers can enrich corporations by paying to drink milk, eat steak, ice cream, cheese, etc. while they develop obesity, diabetes, cancer and heart disease among other things.

According to experts at both Cornell and Harvard, the optimal amount of meat in the healthy human diet is precisely zero.

Reducing meat and dairy consumption by 10% can feed 100 million hungry, malnourished people. Eliminating the meat and dairy based diet will end human starvation on Earth.

Farming sentient individuals is notoriously wasteful when compared to growing plants to feed humans directly. "Livestock" animals, individuals raised for meat and dairy, take drastically more food from the global food supply than they provide, creating shortages for the most vulnerable humans. The amount of crops necessary to feed farmed individuals raised for human food is a vastly larger amount of crops than it would take to feed humans directly.

Thirteen pounds of grain yield just one pound of deceased animals. Crops such as soy and lentils produce, pound for pound, as much protein as animals - sometimes more - without the unsustainable usage of water and land, and pollution of air, water and land.

One acre of land can yield between twelve and twenty times more plant-based food than animal-based food, resulting in the opportunity for more equitable use of food and scarce resources worldwide.

Water is a very precious commodity. 'Water Wars' are predicted for the future! Underground aquifers that took millions of years to fill are running dry. The current use of water necessary to produce the meat and dairy based diet is unsustainable worldwide. It takes copious amounts of water to raise and slaughter exploited individuals. Most of this water is used to flush out and clean up after slaughter (aka. legally accepted murder). Even more water is needed for dairy. At the same time, many human individuals worldwide are experiencing severe and life-threatening water shortages.

Feeding much of the world's edible grain crop and exorbitant amounts of water to unjustly incarcerated farmed individuals while vulnerable humans starve, are malnourished, or without water, is not only inexcusable injustice, but also a grossly inefficient and unsustainable use of natural resources, while simultaneously creating mounting pollution and global warming problems.

"The Earth can produce enough for everyone's need, but not enough for everyone's greed." Mahatma Ghandi

Chapter 15 Climate Change and You

Climate Change, global warming, is threatening our home planet Earth, in unprecedented ways. Warmer temperatures are melting polar ice caps and mountain glaciers causing increases in sea levels. These rising waters are destroying small island nations and eroding coastal areas. Tsunamis, hurricanes, earthquakes, droughts, and floods as well as rising water, have been scientifically linked to climate change caused by greenhouse gasses. The main source of climate changing greenhouse gasses is methane from the meat and dairy based diet, not carbon dioxide from the lack of sustainable energy.

Methane traps heat in the atmosphere much more effectively than carbon dioxide. It is the meat and dairy based diet which is directly responsible for the impending disaster we are currently facing. Rainforests being cut and burned down to provide grazing land and land to grow crops to feed to animals raised for food, also contributes to climate change.

There is a deep injustice in climate change. Rich countries grow richer, while causing the problem. The poorest countries are the most affected and have the least responsibility for the cause. Individuals in the developed world who have access to fossil fuel transportation and the meat and dairy based diet, are emitting the most greenhouse gasses. While those in the developing world eating a low-cost plantbased diet, and walking as a means of transportation, are at most risk of rising water from melting polar ice caps. Some individuals are benefiting at the expense of others.

Food, water, and security issues are execrated by the droughts and floods brought on by global warming. This is especially devastating for the Small Island Developing Nations (SIDN). Rising sea levels make SIDN uninhabitable, as is happening now in the Marshal Islands. People whose families have lived there for generations are being forced to leave by rising waters. In addition, people in these vulnerable situations face the double dilemma of rising sea levels and rising health care costs as they transition away from traditional plant-based diets to the western meat and dairy diet to reflect their upward mobility and develop heart disease, cancer and diabetes.

Climate change is about choices – our choices – because global warming is directly linked to human behavior. Animals raised for food do more to cause global warming and put innocent individuals at risk of hunger and disease than any other source.

The massive amount of animal feces produced in factory farms is the largest source of airborne methane in the United States. Methane traps heat in the atmosphere almost 100 times more effectively than carbon dioxide does. Animals raised for food in the United States produce 130 times more excrement than the entire human population does – 86,000 pounds per second. A typical pig factory generates a quantity of raw waste equal to that of a city of 50,000 people, but without the sewage system. The runoff from factory farms pollutes rivers and lakes more than all other industrial sources combined.

Of all agricultural land in the U.S., nearly 80% is used to raise animals for food. More than 260 million acres of U.S. forest have been cleared to create cropland to grow grain to feed farmed animals. Forests have a cooling effect on the earth, which is lost when they are cut down to provide crops or grazing for cattle.

Twenty times more land is required to feed a meat-eater than to feed a vegan. Raising animals for food consumes nearly half the water used in the U.S. It takes 2,500 gallons of water to produce a pound of beef, but only 25 gallons to produce a pound of wheat. Chicken, hog, and cattle excrement have polluted 35,000 miles of rivers in 22 states, and contaminated groundwater in 17 states.

More than one third of all the raw materials, and non-renewable fossil fuels used in the

United States, are required to raise animals for food. This includes fuel to produce fertilizer for the crops that are fed to animals, oil to run the trucks that take them to slaughter, electricity to freeze their carcasses, and much more. These flesh and blood, sentient creatures are killed in ways that would horrify any compassionate person.

Climate Change has far reaching consequences which most people do not even think about. A hotter world is a hungrier, dirtier, more violent world!

The meat and dairy based diet is not only the main cause of climate change, but also causes world hunger and starvation. More than 80% of starving and hungry children live in countries where food is grown and exported to feed animals raised for food. More than 45% of earth's total land is devoted to raising animals for food. 3.5 billion more people could be fed by growing plants for human consumption on land currently used to grow crops for farmed animals.

And it is dirty! The meat industry causes more water pollution in the United States than all other industries combined. Animals raised for food produce 130 times more excrement than the entire human population, but without the sewage system!

Animals raised for food are the number one cause of wildlife habitat loss, and species extinction. Wild animals are expected to lose 2/3 of their population by 2020. The largest number of exploited, tortured, murdered individuals on earth today are animals: domestic or wild, in the air, on land, and in the water.

This issue of global warming is being addressed on the world stage. There have been several important United Nations initiatives on this dilemma.

No one can argue with the ideas discussed in the United Nations Climate Ambition Summit (December 12, 2020) five years

after the Paris Agreement. Coal consumption needs to be cut, dependence on fossil fuel needs to end, solar, wind, and hydro energy need to be promoted. BUT THE SINGLE GREATEST CONTRIBUTOR TO CLIMATE CHANGE, METHANE FROM ANIMALS RAISED TO BE EATEN BY HUMANS, WAS NOT EVEN MENTIONED.

"Eat less meat" was the personal recommendation of Rajendrak Pachsuri, Chairman of the Intergovernmental Panel on Climate Change (IPCC) and end note speaker of the United Nations Annual Department of Public Information (DPI) Non-Governmental Organizations (NGO) Conference on Climate Change, held at the United Nations in New York a few years ago.

This UN Conference focused on the urgent challenge of global climate change, its causes from human activities, and our collective and individual responsibility in addressing its potentially devastating effects.

Global climate change was discussed as a transformative issue that challenges environment versus economy and presents an opportunity to break with the past. It has become evident that what is needed is a radical change of behavior and consciousness. There needs to be a change in human values, hearts, and minds. We need a light carbon footprint – a reduction of greenhouse gasses. We need to harness more benign sources of energy. According to Thomas Edison in 1931, "The Sun is the greatest source of energy." We need to plant more trees, and we need to eat less meat. Neither of which is happening.

According to a U.N. Food and Agriculture Organization report, Livestock's Long Shadow, recent findings have left no doubt that the warming of the climate is directly linked to human activity. Warmer climate is caused by carbon dioxide and methane – greenhouse gases in the atmosphere resulting from transportation, energy, mechanized farming, and deforestation, among other causes. Of all the causes, the livestock sector generates the most greenhouse gas emissions.

UN System Standing Committee on Nutrition (UNSCN) focuses on Climate Change and Nutrition. The meat and dairy based diet produces methane which traps heat in the atmosphere more effectively than carbon dioxide, and contributes more to global warming than the transportation industry. In April 2017, UNSCN organized a panel on "Climate Change and Nutrition". The panel presented findings on climate change, diets, nutrition and health. Previously explored linkages between climate change and nutrition revealed that projected temperatures increases, changes in precipitation patterns and the frequency of extreme weather events, would lead to reduced agricultural productivity. The link between climate change and nutrition has not received adequate attention by the international community.

Today's global food system is not sufficient, leaving about 800 million people hungry, 2 billion micronutrient deficient, more than

600 million people obese and 2 billion overweight. It is also one of the main contributors to climate change and environmental degradation. Food production and consumption is responsible for 19 – 29 per cent of all human caused greenhouse gas emissions, up to 70 per cent of the freshwater use, and over 60 per cent of the terrestrial biodiversity loss, with animal-based foods being major contributors to these environmental changes. Dietary changes towards more animal-based diets and highly processed food can increase agricultural and food greenhouse gas emissions by up to 80 per cent by 2050.

It is my hope that the information in this Chapter will help you to recognize that global issues are not beyond our grasp but are the direct result of the choices we make. Those choices affect not only ourselves but many, many others who are both vulnerable and innocent. Please think of them as you transition from the unhealthy meat and dairy based diet to a new Plant-Based, sustainable, responsible, and rewarding Lifestyle.

Chapter 16 From Livestock's Long Shadow

'Livestock's Long Shadow - Environmental Issues and Options'. "The Environmental costs per unit of livestock' is a report by the United Nations Food and Agriculture Organization (FAO).

"Livestock is a major threat to the environment. Remedies are urgently needed."

"Which causes more greenhouse gas emissions, rearing cattle or driving cars? Surprise!"

"According to a new report published by the United Nations Food and Agriculture Organization, the livestock sector generates more greenhouse gas emissions as measured in CO_2 equivalent – 18 percent – than transport. It is also a major source of land and water degradation."

"Says Henning Steinfeld, Chief of FAO's Livestock Information and Policy Branch and senior author of the report: "Livestock are one of the most significant contributors to today's most serious environmental problems. Urgent action is required to remedy the situation."

"With increased prosperity, people are consuming more meat and dairy products every year. Global meat production is projected to more than double from 229 million tonnes in 1999/2001 to 465 million tonnes in 2050, while milk output is set to climb from 580 to 1043 million tonnes."

"The global livestock sector is growing faster than any other agriculture sub-sector. It provides livelihoods to about 1.3 billion people and contributes about 40 percent to global agriculture output. For many poor farmers in developing countries livestock are also a source of renewable energy for draft and an essential source of organic fertilizer for their crops."

"But such rapid growth exacts a steep environmental price, according to the FAO report, 'Livestock's Long Shadow – Environmental Issues and Options'. "The Environmental costs per unit of livestock production must be cut by one half, just to avoid the level of damage worsening beyond its present level, it warns."

"When emissions from land use and land use change are included, the livestock sector accounts for 9 percent of CO_2 deriving from human-related activities but produces a much larger share of even more harmful greenhouse gases. It generates 65 percent of human-related nitrous oxide, which has 296 times the Global Warming Potential (GWP) of CO_2. Most of this comes from manure."

"And it accounts for respective 37 percent of all human induced methane (23 times as warming as CO_2), which is largely produced by the digestive system of ruminants, and 64 percent of ammonia, which contributes significantly to acid rain."

"Livestock now use 30 percent of the earth's entire land surface, mostly permanent pasture but also including 33 percent of the global arable land used to producing feed for livestock, the report notes. As forests are cleared to create new pastures, it is a major driver of deforestation, especially in

Latin America where, for example, some 70 percent of former forests in the Amazon have been turned over to grazing."

Land and Water

"At the same time herds cause wide-scale land degradation, with about 20 percent of pastures considered as degraded through overgrazing, compaction and erosion. This figure is even higher in the drylands where inappropriate policies and inadequate livestock management contribute to advancing desertification".

"The livestock business is among the most damaging sectors to the earth's increasingly scarce water resources, contributing among other things to water pollution, eutrophication and the degeneration of coral reefs. The major polluting agents are animal wastes, antibiotics and hormones, chemicals from tanneries, fertilizers and the pesticides used to spray crops. Widespread overgrazing disturbs water cycles, reducing replenishment of above and below ground water resources. Significant amounts of water are withdrawn for the production of feed."

"Livestock are estimated to be the main inland source of phosphorous and nitrogen contamination of the South China Sea, contributing to biodiversity loss in marine ecosystems."

"Meat and dairy animals now account for about 20 percent of all terrestrial animal biomass. Livestock's presence in vast tracts of land and its demand for feed crops also contribute to biodiversity loss; 15 out of 24 important ecosystem services are assessed as in decline, with livestock identified as a culprit."

The Livestock's Long Shadow Report by the
United Nations Food and Agriculture Organization (FAO) does not take into consideration the immense suffering of the innocent individuals who are exploited to provide their precious bodies for human consumption, or the heart disease, diabetes, cancer and obesity in those humans who eat them.

Chapter 17 Sustainable Use of Resources and the SDGs

We may not like to admit it, but we are living on a planet with limited resources. We all want fossil fuel to last forever, but by its very nature, it is limited. That is not a problem for us! We will all switch to solar, wind, and biofuel for energy. Is that a realistic assumption?

What about water? The wars of the past were fought over oil; the wars of the future may be fought over water. Are we hopelessly polluting the water resources we have? How are we using the limited amounts of water we have? More water is used to produce a pound of meat than a pound of grain. Raising animals for food consumes nearly half the water used in the United States. It takes 2,500 gallons of water to produce a pound of beef, but only 25 gallons to produce a pound of wheat.

What about pollution of the water resources we have? The United States Environmental Protection Agency (US EPA) reports that chicken, hog, and cattle excrement have polluted 35,000 miles of rivers in 22 states, and contaminated groundwater in 17 states. The meat industry causes more water pollution in the US than all other industries combined. Animals raised for food produce 130 times more excrement than the entire human population does – 86,000 pounds per second. A typical pig factory farm generates a quantity of raw waste equal to that of a city of 50,000 people, but without the sewage system.

What about energy? We may be trying to move in the direction of sustainable energy slowly but surely, but are we using what we have wisely? More energy is used for the meat and dairy based diet than the more sustainable plant-based diet. Raising animals for food requires more than one third of all the raw materials and fossil fuels used in the United States. This is for fuel to produce fertilizer for crops that are fed to animals, oil to run the trucks that take them to slaughter, electricity to freeze their deceased bodies, and much more.

Isn't it time to think about the fragile quality of life on Earth, and start using our limited resources wisely? The single most important thing anyone can do to promote the wise use of resources is to transition to a plant-based lifestyle for your own health, for justice for the oppressed, and for a more sustainable use of resources.

The United Nations created the Millennium Development Goals (MDGs) at the turn of this century. Then in 2015, the UN moved on to the Sustainable Development Goals (SDGs). They are the following:

1 No Poverty

2 Zero Hunger

3 Good Health and Well-Being

4 Quality Education

5 Gender Equality

6 Clean water and sanitation

7 Affordable and Clean energy

8 Decent work and Economic growth

9 Industry, Innovation, and Infrastructure

10 Reduced Inequality

11 Sustainable Cities and Communities

12 Responsible Production and Consumption

13 Climate Action

14 Life Below Water

15 Life on Land

16 Peace and Justice

17 Partnerships to Achieve the Goal

The plant-based lifestyle is an innovative approach to achieving the Sustainable Development Goals, and a simple solution to reducing climate change, hunger and poverty, improving food security and nutrition, promoting sustainable agriculture, improving human health, using water wisely, improving sanitation, promoting sustainable consumption, and achieving justice for all inhabitants of planet Earth.

Left unchecked, the global demand for meat, eggs, and milk is expected to double from 2000 to 2050 and will have a major impact on land, water and energy use globally. The global issues we face, specifically the unsustainability of the meat and dairy based diet, its impact on human health, (cancer, heart disease, diabetes) the health of this planet (climate change, pollution), and the welfare of our fellow travelers on spaceship earth (the animals) needs to be addressed.

The seriousness of this situation calls for a major step in addressing the issue. Vegan International, a United Nations (UN) Economic and Social Council (ECOSOC) Non-Governmental Organization (NGO), is promoting a UN Convention Against Speciesism. This would follow the United Nations Conventions Against Genocide, Torture, Elimination of Discrimination Against Women (CEDAW) and Rights of the Child. This should be created to insure that all aspects of sustainability are taken into consideration, and that all individuals on earth are taken into consideration and treated justly.

Chapter 18 Effects of Animal Exploitation on the Human Population and the Environment

The exploitation of animals for the meat and dairy based diet is causing the following issues which affect everyone on the planet:

Disease. Zoonotic pandemic disease, such as Covid-19, HIV, Ebola, SARS, MERS, and many others have been linked to 'spill over' from exploited animals to humans, and then are transmitted among humans.

Climate Change. Meat production causes global warming. The massive amount of animal feces produced in factory farms is the largest source of airborne methane in the United States. According to the US Environmental Protection Agency, methane traps heat in the atmosphere more than 20 times more effectively than carbon dioxide does.

Water Pollution. The meat industry causes more water pollution in the United States than all other industries combined. Animals raised for food produce 130 times more excrement than the entire human population does – 86,000 pounds per second. A typical pig factory farm generates a quantity of raw waste equal to that of a city of 50,000 people, but without the sewage system. According to the US Environmental Protection Agency (EPA), the runoff from factory farms pollutes US rivers and lakes more than all other industrial sources combined.

Use of Land. Of all the agricultural land in the United States, nearly 80 percent is used to raise animals for food. More than 260 million acres of United States forest have been cleared to create cropland to grow grain to feed farmed animals. Twenty times more land is required to feed a meat-eater than to feed a plant based vegan.

Use of Water. Raising animals for food consumes nearly half the water used in the United States. It takes 2,500 gallons of water to produce a pound of beef, but only 25 gallons of water to produce a pound of wheat. Also, the US Environmental Protection Agency reports that chicken, hog, and cattle excrement have polluted 35.000 miles of rivers in 22 US states and contaminated groundwater in 17 US states.

Energy. Raising animals for food requires more than one-third of all the raw materials and fossil fuels used in the United States. Satisfying the appetite for flesh requires fuel to produce fertilizer for the crops that are fed to animals, oil to run the trucks that take them to slaughter, electricity to freeze their carcasses, and much more.

Animals. They have complex social and psychological lives, have families, and feel pain as humans do. More than 27 billion animals are killed each year in the United States alone and in horrific ways that would horrify any compassionate person. These individuals are co-inhabitants of planet earth. They deserve rights, a place at the table, and not to be left behind. They are victims of exploitation, murder, species extinction, habitat destruction.

Animal exploitation comes with the accompanying skyrocketing health care costs. The resulting economic burden will be unsustainable in the developing nations.

Dietary Choices, Human Health and Environmental Degradation Are Related: The Plant-Based Lifestyle Equals Healthy People and Healthy Planet.

Chapter 19 Today's Shoah

Alex Hershaft was five years old when the Nazis invaded his native Poland. His father, a prominent chemist, had been invited to work on the Manhattan project. The family was waiting for visas for Alex and his Mother at the time of the invasion.

Almost immediately, half a million Jews were crowded into the Warsaw ghetto. One in five of these individuals died from disease or starvation. Many others were sent to the Treblinka death camp. The remaining people left in the Warsaw Ghetto put up a heroic fight, against impossible odds, to combat the Nazis in their ultimate destruction of the entire ghetto.

Hershaft and his mother survived initially because of the kindness of their gentile, Russian maid. Later they lived on a farm while passing as Christians. After that, it was a Polish orphanage for Alex, followed by five years in an Italian refugee camp. Alex Hershaft emigrated to the United States, and his Mother emigrated to Israel.

His Father is thought to have been caught by the Nazis and killed.

"Why was I spared? Is there a lesson we can learn from this terrible tragedy?"

Dr. Alex Hershaft has a Ph.D. in chemistry, like his Father. He was working as an environmental consultant, specializing in wastewater treatment, when he was sent to a slaughterhouse in the Midwest. Dr. Hershaft turned a corner and saw piles of body parts – hearts, and heads, and hoofs. Horrified, he remembered the extermination camps, and could not get the images out of his mind,

He began to see other similarities between animal agriculture and the death camps in Europe: Farm animals are branded with numbers. They are separated from their families. They are taken to their death in rail cars. They are murdered.

The parallels are not about the victims, but the perpetrators.

According to Hershaft, it was the arbitrary nature of the cruelty that struck him. Their actions are made possible because of arbitrary distinctions that enable cruelty, "The Christian lives, and the Jew dies; the dog lives, and the pig dies."

"You need to get permission from society – to believe that it is alright that one sentient being will live, and another will die." Hershaft says.

Dr. Alex Hershaft is the co-Founder of FARM, 'Farm Animal Rights Movement', the nation's oldest, and the world's first, organization devoted exclusively to promoting the rights of animals not to be raised for food. In addition, he is the Founder of 'A Well Fed World'. He works closely with 'Jewish Veg', an organization that encourages Jews to embrace plant-based diets "as an expression of the Jewish values of compassion for animals, concern for health, and care of the environment."

Why work on behalf of animals when humans suffer?

"Animals are the most defenseless, the most vulnerable, therefore the most oppressed sentient beings on earth. Oppressing animals is the gateway to oppressing humans", says Dr. Hershaft. "Everyone has the awesome power of life and death over animals. Every time we shop for food, we literally make a choice between subsidizing life or subsidizing death".

Dr. Hershaft quotes from the Bible in Deuteronomy, Chapter 30, Verse 19: "I have set before you life and death, blessing and curse. Choose life."

"Eternal Treblinka" is a book by Charles Patterson. The title is from "The Letter Writer", a short story by the Yiddish writer and Nobel Laurate, Isaac Bashevis Singer (1904-91), to whom Patterson's book, "Eternal Treblinka" is dedicated: "In relation to them, all people are Nazis: for the animals it is an eternal Treblinka." The book examines the origins of human supremacy, describes the emergence of industrialized slaughter of both animals and people in modern times, and concludes with profiles of Jewish and German animal advocates on both sides of the Holocaust, including Isaac Bashevis Singer himself.

In the words of Nobel Literature Prize Winner, Isaac Bashevis Singer:

"How much longer, God, will you look on this inferno of yours and keep silent? What need have you of this ocean of blood and flesh whose stench spreads across your universe? Have you created this boundless slaughterhouse merely to show us your power and wisdom?"

"What do they know – all these scholars, all these philosophers, all the leaders of the world – about such as you? They have convinced themselves that man, the worst transgressor of all the species, is the crown of creation. All other creatures were created merely to provide him with food, pelts, to be tormented, exterminated. …for the animals it is an eternal Treblinka."

"THOU SHALT NOT KILL" APPLIES TO ALL OF GOD'S CREATION, NOT ONLY HUMANS.

Chapter 20 United Nations ConventionAgainst Speciesism

Speciesism is exploiting non-human individuals for the sole benefit of the human species. The exploited individuals have no rights of their own. The world needs a United Nations Convention Against Speciesism to stop the injustice of rising water, unsustainable practices, and other cruelties, and provide justice for the exploited.

The global issues we face, specifically the unsustainability of the meat and dairy based diet, its impact on human health, (cancer, heart disease, diabetes) the health of this planet (climate change, pollution), and the welfare of our fellow travelers on spaceship earth (the animals) needs to be addressed by the United Nations in a Convention. A global patchwork quilt approach is not sufficient.

Animal exploitation comes with the accompanying skyrocketing health care costs. The resulting economic burden will be unsustainable in the developing nations. There is a direct relationship between climate change, human health, hunger, sustainable use of resources, pollution, and the exploitation of sentient beings. To protect the defenseless, and reverse the damage this exploitation is causing, there needs to be a new legally enforceable UN Convention.

Animal agriculture and exploitation is the leading cause of pandemics, climate change, resulting, among other things, in the destruction of small island nations and coastal areas; is a major contributor to global pollution of air, water, and land, habit destruction, species extinction, and is a causative factor in many human illnesses including zoonotic diseases such as Covid19, HIV, Ebola, SARS, MERS, Avian and Swine Flu, and many others including heart disease, cancer, diabetes, antibiotic resistance and prevents the accomplishment of the Sustainable Development Goals, specifically Eliminate Poverty and Hunger,

Health and Well-Being, Clean Water and Sanitation, Peace and Justice, Sustainable Oceans.

The slaughter of billions of individuals a year for food, clothing, experiments and entertainment is genocide; exploitive and abusive treatment of sentient individuals of all species is torture, all species have adults – both male and female, as well as children, and should be eligible for the same protection offered in the 1948 United Nations Convention Against Genocide, the 1984 United Nations Convention Against Torture, and the United Nations Convention for the Rights of the Child and the United Nations Convention To Elimination of Discrimination Against Women, (CEDAW).

There is no 'humane' way to slaughter or murder an individual or group; there is no 'humane' way to forcefully collect semen, artificially inseminate, and impregnate, any individuals or group; no family of any species should be forcibly separated; sustainable energy is an efficient and economical alternative for replacing the need for working animals as soon as these alternatives are available; oceans and water bodies need protection from exploitation and forceful removal and diaspora of their residents, and the use of oceans as refuse receptacles. Peaceful co-existence among species is necessary to insure survival of planet Earth, and for the sake of Justice for all.

Unfortunately, not all individuals are in the position to secure their freedom or rights. Sometimes it must be done on their behalf as in President Abraham Lincoln's Emancipation Proclamation which ultimately ended slavery. Vegan International has initiated a United Nations Convention Against Speciesism on behalf of all the abused, victimized, and exploited individuals who currently have absolutely no rights.

"Until we extend out circle of compassion to all living things, humanity will not find Peace." Albert Schweitzer.

Chapter 21 Agriculture: Conventional, Organic and Veganic

The standard American farm model depletes fruit and vegetables of the vitamins and minerals normally found in them and adds toxic chemicals. Almost all the elements in the Chemistry Table of the Elements, are found in soil. They are what is needed for optimal health. Fertilizers and pesticides are poison.

Years ago, there was fear that American farmers would not be able to grow enough food to feed all Americans. A political decision was made to use every inch of farmland to grow crops. The ultimatum was 'Get Big or Get Out!'. Small family farms were forced out of business, and large agricultural entities were formed. The situation has since softened, but the damage is already done.

The standard American agricultural model has one goal – profit. It does not allow the soil to rest and replenish because an empty field does not produce a profit. Instead, fields are repeatedly planted and harvested using heavy applications of fertilizers and pesticides. This is done on both conventional farms and organic farms.

In order to maintain an acceptable level of nutrients, the soil needs to be replenished between crops. It needs to rest and be nourished so that the next crop will have access to the vitamins and minerals which give fruit and vegetables their nutritional value and taste.

Without this natural practice, it is necessary, even for organic farms, to use fertilizers to sustain the new crops. Poisonous pesticides are used to kill the predators who become entrenched, feasting on their favorite crop, and becoming resistant to pesticides. Instead of putting in a crop that predators do not like so they would leave, stronger poisons or more poison are used. Organic farms use the mandated organic fertilizers and pesticides.

Crop rotation does not exist in standard

American agriculture or in Organic agriculture. It involves leaving one field empty. This reduces profit, so it is not used. This focus on profit robs produce of valuable nutrients and the use of pesticides increases the health hazards inherent in eating this produce.

I graduated from the Organic Growers School of the Carolina Farm Stewardship Program when I had a Vegan Retreat and Veganic Farm near Asheville, North Carolina. There an Organic Certifier from Clemson University told me that he goes to an Indian reservation to certify their organic crops. He said there is not a single bug there, and they do not use any pesticides; they rotate the crops.

The widespread routine use of manure as fertilizer, and irrigation with contaminated water is a real concern. Salmonella and E. coli can spread to vegetables and contaminate them. Pathogen runoff from intense animal imprisonment can permeate human water supplies leading to bacterial contamination of rivers and streams impacting both humans and wildlife. These pathogens include fecal coliforms, Streptococcus, Campylobacter, Giardia, Cryptosporidium, E. coli, as well as viruses, all resulting from the unjust exploitation of other species.

What is Organic? It is a method of agriculture that requires adhering to certain rules and regulations. For example, the soil cannot have been previously used for standard farming for a certain number of years. It requires extensive record keeping, which is checked on a regular basis by an Organic Certifier. Fertilizers and pesticides are allowed, just like any other commercial farm, except that only certain 'organic' products can be used. These can be just as poisonous as standard agricultural products. And they are used liberally.

Is organic really better than conventional produce? Let's look at their fertilizers. Conventional farmers like to go to slaughterhouses and take feces and other byproducts of slaughter to use as fertilizer.

Organic farmers do this also, but they take it from organic slaughterhouses. It is still feces, and full of toxic bacteria.

What is the difference between organic livestock and inorganic livestock? They eat different food. The conditions under which they live, and die are the same, but the additives in their food, and the day of slaughter are different.

What is the difference between slaughtering an animal that is inorganic and organic? Usually the day of the week. Organic individuals are slaughtered on Mondays after the slaughterhouse has been cleaned and closed for the weekend. Inorganic individuals are slaughtered after the feces and other hazardous waste has already accumulated. That's what organic patrons are paying extra for – recordkeeping and the day of the week the individuals are murdered.

The extra money you pay for organic produce does not cover healthful additions to the produce. It pays for the time it takes to keep the extensive records, it pays for the

Certifier's time and travel expense to check the records, and finally it pays for all the fertilizers and pesticides, all of which have their own problems.

Fortunately, there is an alternative to conventional or organic agriculture. It is Veganic Agriculture! This is the optimum, most healthful, most sustainable, and most compassionate form of agriculture. It is also the most profitable. The gross income is less because some fields are resting, but because there are no expensive inputs of poisonous pesticides or fertilizers, so the net income is more. There produce is full of vitamins and minerals and not pesticides and fertilizers.

Veganic Agriculture uses no animal inputs. There is no risk of disease or antibiotic resistance from the unsafe substances that the animals are forced to take so that they do not perish from the horrendous conditions they are forced to endure. There is no disease filled animal manure.

A Veganic Farm is a form of sustainable agriculture which uses no animal inputs for soil fertility. Instead, it uses green manures. This is a method of farming which employs crop rotations, cover crops, veganic compost, and imaginative and creative uses of green manures. Some are plowed under, some are killed and left on the surface of the soil for crops to be planted into, and some are planted between rows. Different green manures offer different benefits to the soil. Soil fertility is key to nutritious food since crops take their nutritional value from the soil. Tasteless fruits and vegetables indicate that they have been grown in depleted soil. Soil that is depleted cannot product crops that have vitamins, minerals, and taste. All elements found on the Periodic Chart of the Elements are needed for the human body. All except a few are found in soil. The other few are in the air. You cannot have good health unless you have healthy soil.

Crops are rotated and some fields are left empty (fallow). The empty fields are amended (planted) with cover crops. These are crops rich in nitrogen and other essential nutrients. They grow and develop nitrogen and other essential nutrients. Then they are plowed under to enrich the soil with vitamins, minerals, micronutrients. This rich source of nitrogen provides nourishment for the next crop without the need of expensive fertilizers.

Pesticides are not used or needed either. By the time a predator finds the crop it is looking for, the crop has already been harvested. There is no need for expensive poisonous pesticides.

Veganic farming uses no manure, blood, or bone meal from factory farms and slaughterhouses as is typically used in organic farming. Pests are managed first through crop rotation. Then the philosophy, "Know your Enemy", involves diagnosing the pest or disease. Its life cycle is analyzed to find the vulnerable point. Next the philosophy, "My Enemy's Enemy is my Friend", is employed, and a predator is found that can control situation at that vulnerable point. This eliminates the need for toxic pesticides, even the "natural" poisons used in organic farming. Veganic farming relies on the use of harmless soaps and ashes for pest control.

The widespread routine use of manure as fertilizer, and irrigation with contaminated water in conventional and organic agriculture is a real concern. Salmonella and E. coli from animal feces used as fertilizer can spread to vegetables produced from both conventional and organic methods and contaminate them. Veganic agriculture uses no animal inputs. Instead, it uses 'green manure' - plowed under nitrogen rich cover crops.

The end result of veganic farming is produce that is rich in vitamins, minerals, and flavor, has none of the unhealthy toxic fertilizers and pesticides used in conventional or organic agriculture, no hormones or antibiotics from animal manures and inputs as used in conventional and organic farming, has a light carbon footprint, is globally sustainable, and is totally cruelty free, and that is the best part!

According to Mona Seymour, Associate Professor of Urban and Environmental Studies, Loyola Marymount University:

"Industrial chemical-based agriculture is one of the most destructive human activities on the planet, linked to harmful effects on biodiversity, environmental quality, and farmworker health. Alternative agricultural paradigms avoid chemical inputs yet often rely on animal byproducts sourced from industrial agriculture, such as blood meal and manure. These byproducts are tied to a spectrum of issues, such as potential environmental contamination from veterinary pharmaceuticals and the presence of animal pathogens transmittable to consumers (e.g, E. coli). How do we avoid these problems and grow healthy vegetables, grains, and other plant foods that do not financially or symbolically support industrial agriculture and animal exploitation? Veganic agriculture represents a way forward."

"As the ethical, environmental, and personal health arguments for plant-based diets become increasingly recognized, the demand for food produced without animal inputs is expected to rise. In addition to offering truly plant-based food options to vegans, veganic agriculture has the potential to provide regenerative and agroecological solutions to leading food system issues, including resource depletion, environmental destruction, and foodborne illness related to animal byproducts."

"Today, veganic growing, also known as vegan organic or stock-free organic farming, is a fringe practice in the US. Based on data collected by one of this project's researchers, it is thought that there are approximately 50 commercial veganic farms in the US. However, research trials in the US and UK have shown veganic methods to be viable, with yields similar to organic agriculture, and sources suggest that it is a sustainable form of agriculture."

Chapter 22
The Politics of Food

Today in the United States, the cost of the meat and dairy based diet is kept artificially low by the use of American tax-payer dollars. This is done in the form of "Subsidies." In addition, US tax-payer dollars allow ranchers to leave hundreds of innocent animals out in snow blizzards, hurricanes, and other impossible situations in which they perish, without giving it a second thought, because they know that the US government will 'compensate' them for their 'economic loss'.

How is this accomplished? Billions of dollars in subsidies and compensation are provided to animal agriculture every year by Politicians who prefer not to address the impact of animal agriculture on human health, the environment, or defenseless innocent animals. These Lawmakers continue to provide taxpayer funded subsidies to the unhealthy and environmentally destructive meat and dairy industry in return for contributions to their political campaigns.

The U.S. government spends up to $38 billion each year subsidizing the meat and dairy industries. Less than one percent of that is allocated to assist the production of fruits and vegetables. Most of the agricultural subsidies go to farmers of livestock – the large scale meat and dairy producers, and a handful of major crops, including corn, soybeans, wheat, rice, and cotton, with payments skewed toward the largest producers.

These large-scale crop producers do not follow sustainable agriculture practices. Instead, they use heavy applications of dangerous fertilizers and pesticides which would be unnecessary if they did not try to squeeze as much profit as possible out of every inch of their land. An old- fashioned expression for this would be 'penny wise and pound foolish'. It places immediate profit over long term sustainability with US

Government tax- payer dollars fueling the fiasco, and is completely devoid of concern for human health, the wellbeing of sentient beings, and sustainability of the planet.

Corn and soy inputs used to feed incarcerated animals are heavily subsidized with US taxpayer dollars. These crops are used in the production of meat and processed food by some of the world's largest and richest meat and dairy corporations. Multibillion- dollar corporations hardly need the taxes of hard working, often struggling individual Americans to supplement their profits.

The farm subsidy programs offer financial protection against adverse fluctuations in revenues and production, purchase insurance, pay for marketing, export sales expenses, and research and development. Shoppers pay artificially lower prices at the checkout counter, while their tax dollars fund major meat operations and advertising. Meanwhile, meat and dairy producers accrue yearly retail sales to the tune of 250 billion dollars!

In addition to the political subsidies to the meat and dairy industries, Americans pay for meat and dairy consumption through compromised human health, rising healthcare costs, pollution of land, air, and water, climate disruption involving rising temperatures, rising waters globally, and severe weather incidents such as hurricanes and tornados.

"Meatonomics" by David Simon explains that consumers pay an estimated $2 of invisible costs for every $1 of product the meat and dairy industry sells. By these calculations, a $4 Big Mac actually costs society $12.

The impact of meat consumption is not limited to US borders. A recent report by the United Nations Food and Agriculture Organization (UN FAO), states that agricultural subsidies in economically advanced countries such as the United States artificially depress international market prices forcing poorer nations to import food.

Farmers in the developing world are then forced to leave the market because they can't afford to grow local crops, or feed their families. UN FAO reports that eliminating agricultural subsidies in the U.S. alone would lift millions of people out of poverty worldwide.

At the same time meat subsidies have incentivized the average U.S. citizen to consume about 200 pounds of meat a year. This is more than twice the global average, and nearly twice as much as Americans ate in 1961.

U.S. Government political subsidies are not limited to meat and dairy, they include other individuals capable of feeling pain and suffering – fish. If humans continue fishing at the current levels, research published in "Science" predicts the collapse of all targeted fish species by 2048. Already more than half of the ocean's surface is impacted by industrial fishing. This is an area approximately four times the landmass covered by agriculture. Billions of dollars in government subsidies underly this phenomenon. The United States, Japan, Spain, China, and South Korea provide the largest subsidies to their fishing fleets. Without these subsidies, the fishing industry would not be viable.

Destroying the planet, the lives of innocent sentient individuals, and human health can be very profitable for some politically astute individuals!

The question is: when will US citizens acknowledge the cognitive dissonance around meat consumption, and end subsidy programs that benefit unsustainable animal agriculture in favor of public programs that promote fruits, vegetables, and other plantbased proteins and stimulate a more sustainable food culture?

The United States Environmental Protection Agency (US EPA) instituted mandatory reporting of greenhouse gas emissions across its agencies. However, Congress mysteriously defunded the program to track livestock emissions. Modern animal agriculture is a predominant driver of the climate crisis. Meat and other animal derived products constitute the third-largest source of greenhouse gas emissions globally, following the energy and industrial sectors. Animal agriculture has a larger carbon footprint than the world's entire transportation sector—every car, ship, train, and airplane on Earth. No tangible action is being taken politically to deal with this impending disaster as long as the deep pockets of animal agriculture and commercial fishing are in the picture.

A landmark UN report warned that maximum yield from fisheries could decline another 24 percent by the end of the century if business and emissions proceed as usual. This decimation will occur while the world attempts to double food production by 2050 to sustain the growing human population. Food choices, and the policies we implement to regulate those choices, have dire implications on whether life on land or sea is sustainable or collapses.

The billions of animals bred and raised for food, who do not vote, or have any pockets, never mind deep pockets, endure mutilation, genetic manipulation, and unsanitary and tightly confined conditions in modern animal agriculture because their misery is shielded from the public by the animal agriculture-backed "Ag-Gag" legislation. This legislation makes it illegal to filming or otherwise expose conditions in animal agriculture. The purpose of "Ag-Gag" legislation is to prevent animal agriculture's loss of revenue from those consumers who would be put off from knowing the truth about where their meat comes from. This legislation is accomplished with money paid in political contributions to those in power who can create and enforce it.

Political changes do not need to make animal rights or welfare a focal point. The end of government subsidies for animal agriculture make sense for many other reasons including human health, environmental concerns. Policymakers have ample reason to incentivize the growth of plant-based foods.

Ending subsidies for meat production and pointing consumers in the direction of healthy, sustainable plant based foods would be an effective policy. A subsidy removal by another name (behavioral taxes) has a proven track record of nudging people away from products like sugary drinks and tobacco towards other goods that achieve positive social impact.

Consumers in the United States would save copious amounts of money during their lifetimes if plant-based programs were implemented according to Economist's projections. Oxford University economic projections indicate that removal of animal flesh and secretions from the global food system could save over a trillion dollars in environmental costs in the next 30 years.

Removing animal agriculture political subsidies from meat, dairy, sea animals, and products derived from them would mean that those human individuals who choose to consume these other individuals would be paying the more accurate costs of their decisions which affect the health of everyone including the planet at large. Big agriculture has significant lobbying power and political clout to deter elected officials from sustainable actions, however this does not diminish the ethical necessity of voters to push for change.

Some suggestions for political activists are to influence elected officials to encourage support for smaller farming productions and help to retrain livestock farmers. Equity should be encouraged. The larger the producer, the fewer tax-payer subsidies it should receive, the smaller the farm or company, the higher the percentage of subsidies. Doing this would break down the power structure of large meat and dairy corporations and prop up sustainable locally based agriculture.

Political involvement to accomplish these goals will move the emphasis of food production, and its profits, away from factory farming and to small-scale farms owned and operated by the very working people who have long been marginalized by the big animal agriculture machine. The transition to sustainable agriculture should include appropriate investment allocated toward regenerative and veganic farming training programs that implement procedures that do not use harmful and dangerous fertilizers and pesticides and that maintain soil fertility without damaging local wildlife.

Subsidies should be reallocated to the production of plant-based foods. Such a rearranging of subsidies would incentivize Americans to eat more sustainable and healthy foods, and allow farmers and small businesses to produce crops at lower prices for consumers, in turn lifting up half of the country which currently struggles with food security. Low- income communities are often made to consume cheaply made, highly processed fast-foods such as hot dogs and hamburgers due to limited access to grocery stores with affordable fresh and nutritious options as well as insufficient public transportation. Our current meat and dairy subsidy programs only exacerbates this issue. By investing political subsidies in the production of whole plant-based foods instead, we can begin to shift the negative health impacts experienced by vulnerable low-income groups toward diets that are more healthful and environmentally sustainable.

Ideally there should be a national education program highlighting the health and economic benefits of plant-based nutrition, as well as the political solutions. Both Public Health and Human Services Departments and grass-roots pressure on Elected Officials are necessary to achieve a reversal of damage done by past political policies

Public schools which currently insist on students taking containers of milk regardless of whether or not they drink it, should stop this extremely detrimental practice. Instead, educational information should be provided on dietary choices that do not include meat and dairy. Vegan alternatives should be provided every day in public school cafeterias. This is an invaluable component to changing the direction of American behavior regarding food choices.

Corporate greed in the food industry is the root cause of the negative effects of meat and dairy on human health, climate change, and pollution of air, land, and water. If constituents lobby their legislators to remove the unjustly spent taxpayer dollars from the lucrative animal exploitation industry, it would allow the price of meat to rise to its actual cost. Not only would this affect the United States, but would reduce hunger and starvation in developing nations exporting their produce to feed unjustly incarcerated livestock while they and their children are hungry or starving.

US Citizens could then make healthier choices based on economics as well as scientific facts. The end result would be reduction of preventable illness, such as diabetes, heart diseases, and some cancers in the United States, and reduction of poverty, hunger and starvation in the developing nations. In addition, pollution, species extinction, habitat destruction, zoonotic disease, land degradation and desertification, global warming would be reduced significantly. Most importantly, it would eliminate the suffering of innocent individuals of other species who currently have no protection against exploitation, while changing the trajectory of Earth's current unsustainable trajectory for future generations.

Chapter 23 Dairy Is Scary

If you have ever seen a man who needs a bra, or encountered one that has no testicles, then you experienced first-hand the results of the dairy industry. This is nothing compared to the experiences of those innocent individuals incarcerated, exploited, and executed by the dairy industry. Hence the motto: 'Dairy is Scary'.

In the camps in Europe in the 1940's, during the separations/selections, young women with babies in their arms were told to give the baby to their own Mother, the child's Grandmother. This gave the impression that the baby would be safe, taken care of, and that they would be reunited with the baby again. The young mothers were then sent to 'work', aka slave labor. They never saw their babies or Mothers (the Grandmothers) again. The young women who had no one to give their baby to, were sent with their baby, directly to their deaths. It was a known fact that there was no incentive to live for Mothers after losing their babies.

All species experience the same emotions.

I had a Veganic Retreat and Farm in North Carolina a while ago. My neighbor was a cattle rancher. Every evening after dinner, I went to the fence between our properties and 'visited' with my favorite cow, '717', the number in her ear, and a Brahman Steer, kept as a 'pet', named Larry. He was very tall and would bend his head down like when he eats grass so I could hug his neck. I still have pictures of them. Larry's face is on the Vegan Retreat Twitter account. He was a very handsome guy!

At one point, my neighbor decided to take 717's son to 'auction'. This is a place where the baby bulls and others go to await slaughter. I could hear him kicking like crazy inside the transportation vehicle. His Mother, 717, cried and bellowed and mourned for weeks after that. Her grief was heartbreaking.

After a while, I went to visit her to express my condolences. She came running over toward me. I was concerned that she must view humans as villains – instruments of death - and might retaliate. Knowing her ways from visiting her at the fence in the evenings, I took one step backwards. This is what she does when she is uncomfortable or afraid. She stopped instantly because she knew what it meant. There was no animosity, desire for revenge, or anything negative.

Evidence shows that Dairy is NOT a good source of nutrition. It is a good source of corporate profits at the expense of exploited, abused animals, with no benefit to the human body. Ditch Dairy!

Here is what a well-known Doctor has said about the health consequences of drinking milk:

From "The Case Against Milk" By John Mc Dougall, M.D.

"The milk industry has done a great deal to create and maintain a positive image for milk…A growing body of evidence is proving the hazards of milk consumption really outweigh the benefits…A look at their nutritional content emphasizes that dairy products are not the 'perfect' food. Milk and its products fail to provide adequate amounts of fiber. linoleic acid, iron, vitamin B3 and vitamin C to meet the nutritional needs of adults and children. The nutrients for which milk is touted are easily obtained from vegetable foods, which contain more of the above nutrients as well. The vitamin D with which milk is fortified can be more safely and efficiently obtained from exposure to sunlight."

"Milk is high in fat…fat is a major dietary culprit. Research links it with heart disease, adult onset diabetes, cancers of the breast, colon and prostate, and other serious illnesses…By taking out the fat, you get a product considerably more concentrated in protein. Too much protein in the diet creates other problems, like allergies and calcium leaching…skim milk is not a good alternative choice."

"Milk is the cause of allergy…Gastrointestinal problems – colic (from drinking milk or through the breastmilk of a mother who drinks it), stomach cramps, abdominal distention, bloody stools, colitis, malabsorption, loss of appetite, diarrhea, constipation, irritation of the tongue, lips and mouth."

"Iron deficiency anemia. At least 50% of childhood iron deficiency anemia is from dairy products…and is not responsive to iron therapy until milk and other dairy products are eliminated."

"The extremely allergic person can develop life-threatening anaphylactic shock. Also, in several studies, sudden infant death syndrome (SIDS) has been linked with milk allergy."

"Dairy foods have been implicated in the development of a cancer of the immune system called Hodgkins' disease."

"Some other life-threatening conditions are linked to dairy products. A Department of Health and Social Security Report, and research reported in the British Medical Journal, confirm that adverse reactions to milk can cause several serious disorders. They include congestive heart failure, newborn heart failure (neonatal tetany) from low blood calcium levels triggered by milk's high phosphate levels, tonsil enlargement, lifelong obesity and aggravation of ulcerative colitis."

"Most people cannot digest milk properly…people naturally lose the ability to digest lactose, the carbohydrate found in milk, because they no longer synthesize the digestive enzyme lactase. This condition, known as lactose intolerance, results in symptoms of diarrhea, gas and stomach cramps."

"As with meat, milk picks up and concentrates contaminants such as pesticides, industrial waste, chemicals, heavy metals, steroids and antibiotics. Other chemicals, like DDT, are known carcinogens (cancer causing agents). Breast milk can have dangerously high levels of these substances."

"Dairy products are easily contaminated by disease causing bacteria. Bacteria such as salmonella, staphylococci, E. coli and viruses known to cause leukemia are very much at home in milk…Pasteurization and normal cooking do not kill viruses…Staphylococcal food poisoning occurs most commonly with not-fat dry milk, cheese and butter.

"Dairy products are not the best source of calcium."

"Looking at worldwide statistics it becomes more evident that milk is not a calcium powerhouse. The most rotten teeth and the weakest bones are found in countries where the most dairy products are consumed - United States, Canada, Australia, New Zealand and Scandinavian countries."

"The bottom line is this: calcium deficiency is not a threat to someone eating a diet of whole foods."

"Infants fed dairy products can develop susceptibility to nervous system disorders. A poorly developed nervous system may run the risk of developing the degenerative disease multiple sclerosis later in life.…It is more commonly found in areas of the world where infants and children are raised on dairy products rather than on breast milk and vegetable foods."

"For people who already have multiple sclerosis, removal of animal fats from the diet can have dramatic results."

"Milk does more harm than good for ulcers… British and American patients treated for ulcer disease with dairy products developed two to six times the number of heart attacks at the end of one year as those treated without dairy products."

"No other animal in its natural environment drinks the milk of another species, nor do any drink milk after weaning. We don't have to either. We can better obtain the few nutrients available in dairy foods from fresh whole vegetable foods."

Further, mounting scientific evidence points to milk as a source of disease, not health. Despite no evidence that milk protects against bone fractures and osteoporosis, it continues to be marketed as necessary for bone health. The simple equation of milk = calcium= strong bones is nothing more than smart marketing. Often thought of as the only source of calcium, milk, is a very recent addition to most food cultures. Great sources of plant-based calcium abound and include greens, broccoli, tofu, corn tortillas, nuts and seeds.

Medical studies have found dairy consumption to be linked to a higher risk for various cancers, especially prostate, breast and ovarian cancer, as well as increased sex hormones in children, and early puberty in young girls. Also, the liquid calories and hormones in milk contribute to obesity and diabetes.

When people who are lactose intolerant drink milk, they can experience digestive problems like gastrointestinal distress, diarrhea, and flatulence and impeded nutrient absorption. Lactose intolerance is the norm in most ethnic groups.

In addition, evidence shows that Multiple Sclerosis, Type 1 Diabetes and Osteoporosis are linked to cow's milk. Countries that use the most cow's milk also have the highest fracture rates and the worst bone health.

The main reason for the popularity of dairy is corporate profit. This is why it is in all the school lunch programs where it supports childhood obesity among other things.

From "Farm To Fable" by Robert Grillo, Founder of Free From Harm.

"Our demand for animal products supports a $154.8 billion meat industry that profits from the abject and needless suffering of some ten billion animals annually in the US alone."

"The dairy industry has most people believing that cow's milk, and the cheese, yogurt, butter, ice cream, and other products derived from it, are natural for us to consume. But if these products are indeed so natural, then why is dairy farming based on so many extremely unnatural practices?" "Artificial Insemination"

"To appreciate how euphemistic artificial insemination is when referring to the forced and systematic breeding practices of farmed animals, we must first consider what it means in the case of human beings.

For starters, artificial insemination in female humans is elective, not forced upon them. Next, artificial insemination is seen as a hopeful solution, a good technology that could actually help a couple achieve their lifelong dream of having a family. And finally, insemination is a short, relatively painless procedure that many women describe as being similar to a Pap smear.

But in dairy cows, goats, turkeys, and other farmed animals, the procedure is none of these things. For one thing, it causes clear signs of emotional distress and physical pain. What's worse, the procedures that involve shooting semen into the vagina of female animals and (rectal penetration in cows) are crude, invasive, and often performed by farm workers who have little or no veterinary experience.

AI, as it is called in the industry, is done repeatedly until it is certain that the animal becomes pregnant. After repeatedly birthing, she becomes "spent" and therefore an economic liability to farmers who then send her to slaughter.

All of this is done without the animal understanding why she is being violated or why her offspring are being taken from her. Using artificial insemination to refer to this cruel and perverse assault on farmed animals is a classic example of how euphemisms in animal agriculture function to mask a terrible truth."

Here is an investigative report of a typical dairy farm operation.

"Investigation of a Florida Commercial Dairy Farm", by Animal Recover Mission (ARM)

"Richard 'Kudo' Couto is the Founder, Chief Executive Director and Lead Investigator of The Animal Recovery Mission (ARM). Before ARM's inception in 2010, Kudo was a board member and investigator for the local SPCA. He was responsible for shining the light on illegal animal and horse slaughter farms in South Florida."

"Established in 2010, The Animal Recovery Mission (ARM) is a non- profit investigative organization dedicated to eliminating extreme animal cruelty operations worldwide. Our mission is to be an uncompromising defending force for the welfare of animals in addition to putting an end to and preventing pain, suffering and torture inflicted as a result of inhumane practices."

"ARM did an undercover investigation at a dairy farm located in Okeechobee (Florida). As a part of its animal agriculture and factory farm focus, ARM agents obtained positions as employees in its efforts to unveiling the dark secrets behind the doors of the dairy industry.

What was revealed, shocked even the most seasoned investigators of ARM, and confirmed rumors that the dairy farm is considered to be the most brutal operations of all of the dairy farms in Florida."

"During this investigation, incriminating and disturbing video footage included, but was not limited to the following;"

"The cows are contained in over cramped holding barns during the 305 days a year of the milk production phase. Oftentimes, they overheat and collapse from exhaustion and heat due to the extremely poor living conditions and insufficient ventilation."

"Cows are ridiculed and tormented as they are maneuvered to the milk production lines by the use of electrical prods, withstanding violent and excessive force."

"Cows are beaten into submission with metal construction rods known as rebar. Undercover agents documented several forms of 'home made' torture tools, including a spear-like weapon that is used to repeatedly stab the animal in the ribs, inflicting wounds that are left untreated. They are also beaten over their heads and bodies with these rods."

"As a result of the continuous and forceful beatings, the cows fall to the ground."

"During daily milk collections, the cows are beaten over the head, punched, poked and kicked (including their sensitive udders) with other primitive tools, hooks and tools. The majority of these beatings occur whilst the frightened animals are trapped in a metal headlock and unable to escape. The cows were witnessed to be maliciously beaten repeatedly for no apparent reason and deep wounds and untreated abrasions were evident."

"During milking, workers are taught to grab the cows' tails and forcefully bend/fold and possibly break the tail bones."

"On the dairy farm, milk is collected from the cows three times a day. This means that, the animals are being subjected to major stress, discomfort, pain, torture and suffering three times a day, 360 days of the year. Through this investigation, it is clear that the workers on the farm have an unwavering and deep hatred for the dairy cows and the beatings relay an inferior respect of the animals' welfare and rights to life."

"Outside of the milking and holding barns, the abuse continues with the calves – considered as mere bi-products of the dairy industry. Sadly, the protocols on dairy farms are to rip the babies away from their mother, sometimes as they are born. On the dairy farm, the mistreatment of the newborn calves is evident."

"Frightened, confused and desperate for their mothers these babies are isolated in rickety cramped enclosures, unlike those displayed on the Larson website. Left outside in the harsh environment, laying in mud and their own feces, the calves often face peril from prolonged exposures to the extremities of the weathering heat and inclement weather. If cover is provided, it is in the form of disintegrating, shredded tarps."

"Observed during ARM's extensive investigation, is the close interaction of owner and operator to the treatment to the animals. This included the animal health, treatment and overall care and consideration of the dairy cows upon the dairy farm. On multiple occasions he was found to be either serving or encouraging inhumane acts against the animals that caused unnecessary pain and suffering amongst the dairy cows under his custody and ownership."

"In fact, milking barn #5 (as it is referred to) is under the owner's DIRECT supervision. At no time during this investigation, did he reserve his criminal abusive acts nor did he reprimand or fire employees for the cruelty and maltreatment being executed upon the animals.

Veritably, the opposite actions were produced when one of the former employees (and ARM investigator), who attempted to disclose animal abuse upon this operation, was served instead, with a lawsuit to retract any statements of animal abuse concerns. This is in contradiction of the company's own code of ethics, clearly lined out in the employment contracts."

"ARM goals lie within exposing the dirty secrets that lay behind the walls of conglomerates of animal agriculture business, like the dairy industry. The chain of command and partnerships involved along the way from farmers to producers, distributors, and your local supermarkets, is causing epic animal abuse that occurs every single day."

"With so many alternatives of dairy available in today's society, there is an imminent need to end the cruelty associated within these operations for our own consumption. ARM's message stands to adopt plant-based diets, compassionate lifestyles and to go vegan."

Is 'organic' really better? Here is a firsthand observation:

"I Visited A Small, Organic Dairy Farm to See If Animals Were Treated Better" by Robert Grillo, Founder of Free From Harm.

"While passing a small dairy farm on Sir

Francis Drake Boulevard in the Point Reyes National Seashore in early October, I decided to pull over and have a closer look.

I saw about 60 "heifers" in one large muddy, gated enclosure, up to their ankles in mud and manure. There was a lone calf, probably a male just born to one of the heifers, placed in a holding area where some of the cows were doting over him on the other side of the steel bars of a gate.

To the right of them was a "milking parlor," consisting of an old shed where two men were bringing cows in and out to be milked and hooking up their udders to milking machines.
The cows perked up as I approached the fencing and stared meekly up into my eyes. And to the right of this was a section consisting of rows of small white plastic hutches, each with a single calf inside.

When I pulled up, I saw a gruff yet handsome young man walking toward his tractor. I approached him to ask if I could have a look around the dairy farm. He asked me to wait a minute as he opened the valve to let the oil drain from his tractor.

"You're giving it an oil change," I said.

"Yes," he said, "I'll give that a chance to drain out while I show you around."

"His name was Ernest. I learned that he was the son of a family who owned this 200head dairy farm for many generations, producing all pasture-based, grass-fed, organic milk. Ernest lives in the modest old frame house right across the road from this dairy operation, the same one many generations of his family lived in.

To my surprise, he seemed very receptive to having an impromptu visitor, as he scraped away the manure to create a clear path on the ground for me to walk on leading to the calf crates. He started telling me about the calves before I even had a chance to ask, confirming that the plastic hutches were housing all newborn female calves.

"The males are out of here right away", Ernest explained. "We have someone who comes and picks them up. I have no idea where they go." They must be sold for veal or other kinds of meat, I said. And he nodded in agreement. "The females here are all separated in their own hutch, so if one gets sick, she doesn't get all the others sick too." "This calf licked my hand and wanted to suckle. They should be as playful as puppies, but instead their spirits are already broken and there is a look of hopelessness in their eyes."

"I walked up to the first calf in a hutch and she approached me immediately, licking my hand cautiously through the fence and wanting to suckle. Others just cowered back into their plastic hutches, an expression of hopelessness and loneliness on their little faces.

They were all just days or weeks old, in many ways like large puppies, only instead of bouncing around and wanting to play, their spirits were already broken. You could see it in their eyes. Their mothers were only forty or fifty feet away yet separated by the large milking parlor shed which blocked them from viewing one another.

"Is there anything else you want to know about?" Ernest asked. And so I asked him about artificial insemination. He seemed proud to tell me that he now does AI and breeds the cows himself. AI is farmer talk for forcing one arm all the way up the cow's rectum and shooting a semen gun into her vagina with another. This humiliating violation of her body is performed repeatedly, until it is certain she is impregnated.

"Come on, let me show you something," he said, as he escorted me back to the mini feed lot where the heifers were standing in the mud. He pointed to one of the heifers in heat, which, he said, was indicated by the other female cows trying to mount her. He explained that he could buy the bull semen that guaranteed only females would be born, but that it's too costly to use here."

"I asked him how many cycles of pregnancy they would go through until they were considered "spent." He explained that they keep the cows only as long as they're producing more value in milk than the cost of feeding them. He recalls his grandfather telling him that the younger heifers produce better milk, so the younger, the better.

"It's a really tough business," Ernest confessed. Lots of problems with the cows. Some can't get pregnant; others have complications with pregnancies, like still borns, or they develop diseases like mastitis, lameness, tumors, bovine leukemia and distended udders that look like they are carrying milk but are just full of fat cells. And as they sag, their teats get dirty and this affects the milk. None of these cows are economically viable, so they too, in their frail state, are picked up by the man he hires to take them where he never has been, where they are turned into hamburger."

"All the while Ernest's matter-of-fact, business-like demeanor showed no signs of acknowledging the emotional or physical suffering of the animals in his care. Having grown up in a family of dairy farmers for several generations, it was simply business as usual. As long as customers like Trader Joe's continues to buy his organic, pasture raised, grass fed milk, he'd remain in business, but it was clear that he was just getting by, perhaps one of the few independent dairy farms left in the region, in the country. Dairy farming is all he knows, but if he has sons and daughters, they will most likely find other professions.

As I drove off and looked back in the distance at the farm, it seemed to exist as if a mirage in the midst of a vast desert, a kind of surreal gathering of invasive species in a vast and otherwise pristine coastal wilderness, one of the most diverse and cherished in the world."

Dairy is not only a health and well-being issue and a source of corporate profit, but also an entrenched political issue.

From "Seed the Commons calls on the San Francisco Board of Education to take a stance against school milk" by Nassim Nobari, www.seedthecommons.org.

"Health. Milk has been a cornerstone of American school meals for generations. Mounting scientific evidence points to milk as a source of disease, not health."

"Bone Health. Despite little to no evidence that milk protects against bone fractures and osteoporosis, it continues to be marketed as necessary for growth and bone health. The simple equation of calcium = milk = strong bones is nothing more than smart marketing."

"Cancer. Instead of setting children up for a lifetime of health, medical studies have found dairy consumption to be linked with a higher risk for various cancers, especially prostate, breast and ovarian cancer."

"Hormones. All cow's milk contains bovine hormones, which is thought to explain why milk consumption is linked to an increase of cancers of the reproductive system, as well as increased sex hormones in children and early puberty in young girls."

"Obesity & Diabetes. The liquid calories and hormones in milk contribute to childhood obesity and diabetes. San Franciscans have strongly advocated to reduce liquid calorie consumption, from soda to fruit juice, but milk has remained a blind spot."

"Lactose Intolerance. When people who are lactose intolerant drink milk, they can experience digestive problems like gastrointestinal distress, diarrhea, and flatulence and impeded nutrient absorption. Lactose intolerance is the norm in most ethnic groups."

"Calcium. Often thought of as the only source of calcium, milk is in fact a very recent addition to most food cultures, which have been raising healthy kids without it. Great sources of plant-based calcium abound and include greens, broccoli, tofu, corn tortillas, and nuts and seeds."

"Food Justice. Children have little choice when it comes to drinking milk in San Francisco public schools. With 85% of students being children of color and predominantly lactose intolerant, and many belonging to communities overburdened by obesity and diabetes—some of the same diseases linked to dairy consumption—these pro-dairy school meal policies end up disproportionately harming them."

Dairy cows live short, confined lives of forced births, unnatural feeds, painful injections, and calcium depleted bones. To produce milk, dairy cows must give birth. They produce a calf a year, which is taken from them soon after birth. Mother cows mourn the loss of their baby calves. The cows endure a physically demanding nine month gestation period, during which time they give milk for the first seven months. With genetic mutation, cows produce 100 pounds of milk a day – ten times more than in nature. Their udders are so heavy and swollen that they are in constant pain and are unable to walk properly.

Hormones banned in Europe and Canada are used in the United States to increase milk production. This causes birth defects in the calves. The cows are fed unnatural diets which cause disease, some of which are fatal. All dairy cows suffer from diseases directly related to the way they are treated. In nature, cows live about 20 years, in the dairy industry, they are 'unproductive', spent, and slaughtered at about three or four years old. They are slaughtered in horrific ways, and become low grade hamburger, and low quality beef products.

"Downed cows" are worn out, depleted dairy cows who are so weak, and diseased from the lives they have been forced to live, that they cannot stand. These "downers" are still sold for human consumption. They are typically left without food, water, or care, for days until it is convenient to take them to slaughter. Usually they are moved by the most convenient, least humane ways, such as being dragged or pushed with tractors or forklifts. This causes even more suffering and injuries. Downed animals are not protected from abuse under federal animal welfare laws, no matter how cruel the treatment is.

Veal calves are the by-product of the dairy industry. Male calves are not able to produce milk, so they are taken from their mothers, chained by the neck, and kept in crates so small they cannot turn around, stretch, or lie down. Their muscles are not able to develop, keeping their meat 'tender'. They are fed a poor diet, making them anemic. These sick, abused animals produce pale-colored flesh. These inhumane conditions cause the calves to be more likely to develop diseases than cattle in more normal circumstances. Veal calves require copious amounts of medication to keep them alive until slaughter at a few months of age. Veal is the most likely meat to contain illegal drug residues which pose a threat to human consumption.

Cows are Mothers. They have been forcefully and brutally raped, and their babies stolen from them. They grieve inconsolably for their babies. The boys are brutally slaughtered. The girls are fed a type of formula until they are just barely old enough to become Mothers themselves. Then they are raped, tortured, tormented, and forced to produce milk until their bodies wear out. 'Spent' cows are brutally slaughtered after their short lives filled with endless sorrow and pain. There is a deep injustice in dairy. For your sake and theirs, please don't consume dairy!

Chapter 24
The Truth About Eggs

Eggs are probably the highest source of cholesterol available. Fat and cholesterol have been linked to most diseases including heart disease, diabetes, and cancer.

Cage-free, free-range, and organic are marketing terms used to sell cholesterol laden eggs to consumers who erroneously believe that these eggs are somehow 'healthful' and guilt free. Nothing could be further from the truth.

Eggs are the hens' menstrual period which is unfertilized by roosters because the roosters have all been executed as chicks by huge agribusiness corporations.

Hens lay eggs. Male chicks are of no use to the egg industry. Newborn baby male chicks are thrown into plastic garbage bags. They suffocate slowly under the weight of the other chicks dumped on top of them or are pulverized in machines designed to grind them up alive. Male chicks are also ground up for animal feed while still alive.

The male chicks are not treated any better by the organic, cage-free, free-range, than the conventional egg industry. These unwanted, unprofitable, vulnerable individuals are murdered, often hours after birth, by the same methods as conventional male chicks.

While the male chicks are murdered soon after birth, the female chicks are mutilated by being de-beaked. The sensitive beak, comparable to the human finger-tip, is removed to prevent the babies from committing suicide by pecking themselves to death, which would eliminate profits.

In nature, Mother Hens keep all their baby chicks – boys and girls – safe under their wings until they are old enough to venture out alone.

Huge agribusiness corporations produce eggs, both the conventional and specialty eggs. All hens are kept in crowded battery cages where their most basic instincts are cruelly violated. There is no natural light. There are four or five hens in each cage. They cannot walk or stretch their wings. Their feathers fall out, their skin becomes raw and often bloody, and their feet are injured, and often caught, by the wire floor. When the hen's feet become caught in the wire floor, it can prevent her from reaching food. Hens can slowly starve to death inches from food. Dead hens remain in the cage with living hens.

To prevent cannibalism, hens are debeaked. A hot blade cuts through bone, cartilage, and soft tissue. The beak is as sensitive and as the human finger-tip. Many birds die from shock during the process. The industry uses enormous amounts of antibiotics, pesticides, and other chemicals. Pesticides are fed to the hens so that their excrement attracts fewer flies. Eggs yolks are chemically dyed to achieve a yellow look, which in nature comes from the sun.

When egg production falls off, the industry starves, and denies hens water, for several days. This 'forced molting' shocks the hens into losing whatever feathers they have left, and starts a new egg laying cycle. Many hens die during this tortuous cycle. There is no veterinary care. Dying hens are thrown on 'dead piles' with the dead hens.

Cage Free facilities often house several thousand birds in a single building. They cannot walk around, fly, groom themselves, or engage in any natural behavior. They live in feces and urine, and breath ammonia not air. But they are 'cage free'.

Free range is no better. These caring, affectionate, intelligent beings are not protected by any laws or regulations defining 'free range'. Free range is anything the profit driven producer wants it to be. This is a marketing term used to sell products to uninformed consumers, not a way to treat the hens better.

Organic only refers to the food the birds eat. All other horrific circumstances of their short horrific lives, and inhumane slaughter are the same. Organic is about profit; it is not about compassion or health.

In nature, hens produce approximately ten eggs a year, and only during the breeding season. Commercial egg laying hens are forced to produce up to 300 eggs a year. This is done by forcing a molt, or starving the hens into a new cycle in their bodies.

Eggs can become trapped in the hens' bodies. Since there is never any Veterinary help for these animals, the eggs are 'cooked' in the hens' bodies. This causes the hens to perish in a horrible and painful death.

Hens usually live 10 to 15 years in nature. In the egg industry the hens live 12 to 18 months before their bodies give out.

Hens are sentient beings not protected by the 'Human Slaughter Law'. Those very limited protections are reserved for mammals - animals, who like humans, produce milk for their young. This restriction exists because humans can 'relate' to mammals more than hens.

Birds, and other non-mammals, are slaughtered in the most horrific ways. The focus is on profits, not compassion. These two are mutually exclusive, and no slaughter is 'humane'.

Eggs are neither healthful nor humane. They are a tremendous source of both disease-producing cholesterol and unimaginable cruelty. It is best to avoid them.

Chapter 25
What We Eat Shows Our Courage and Compassion

This book would be remiss without mentioning some intangible aspects of 'Lifestyle'. A Plant-Based Lifestyle is not just about our health and well-being. It is about more than that. It is also about our courage, compassion, and happiness. The Plant-Based Lifestyle requires courage, and determination. It requires courage to make difficult decisions, and determination in implementing, and continuing to implement them. It requires courage to pursue this path, and determination not to give up when others around you do not act compassionately. Plant-Based means eating courageously and compassionately.

Each year more than 5 billion pigs, cows, calves, turkeys, and fish are killed for food in the United States alone. On factory farms where most animals, dairy, and eggs come from, animals are crammed into cages so small that they cannot even turn around.

Babies are taken from mothers, often as soon as they are born. Male chicks in egg facilities are ground up alive for fertilizer or suffocated in plastic bags. Disease is so prevalent in these conditions that antibiotics are routinely fed to animals causing antibiotic resistance in humans, one of the largest threats to human health today.

More chickens, hens and roosters, are farmed than any other animal. Over nine billion chickens are murdered each year. It is approximately one million an hour in the United States alone. The scale of their suffering is unimaginable. Tens of thousands of these individuals are kept in sheds where there is no natural light. The air is unbreathable due to ammonia from urine. Baby chicks have their beaks and toes cut off to prevent fighting due to extreme overcrowding. Debeaking cuts through bone, cartilage, and soft tissue without benefit of pain relief. These sentient being who are raised for meat are genetically altered to grow twice as fast, and twice as large, as normal individuals. This causes multiple health issues and the unhealthy living conditions expose them to all kinds of disease, which can then be transferred to humans. One of these zoonotic pandemics is Avian Flu, but these conditions make many other inter-species pandemic outbreaks possible.

Transportation to slaughter is done by the cheapest means possible. The hens and roosters are packed in crates on the backs of trucks unprotected from weather conditions. Individuals literally freeze to death in winter, or die from heat stress, and suffocation in summer. At the slaughterhouse, which is also referred to as a 'packing' or 'processing' plant, crates of these defenseless individuals are removed from trucks with cranes or forklifts and dumped on a conveyor belt. As the birds are unloaded, some fall on the floor where they die from being crushed by machinery or vehicles, or they die slowly from starvation, and neglect. Fully conscious hens and roosters are hung by their feet on a moving rail. Stunning is not required because they are not covered by the Humane Slaughter Act. These individuals are killed as cheaply as possible, regardless of the additional suffering it causes. The birds' throats are slashed, usually by a mechanical blade which often misses. Then the dead, and the live hens and roosters, are submerged in boiling water. Birds missed by the killing blade are boiled alive. This is such a common occurrence that they are called 'redskins'.

Hen and Tom Turkeys are slaughtered at the rate of about 300 million a year. Most are raised in confinement. Disease and suffering are rampant in these inhumane conditions. Stressed turkeys are driven to fighting, causing 'economic' loss. To prevent 'loss', the turkey's beaks and toes are cut off without pain relief. Turkeys have been anatomically manipulated to grow abnormally fast and large. If a seven-pound baby grew at the same rate as the turkeys are forced to, the baby would weigh 1500 pounds at 18 weeks of age. When the hens and toms reach market weight, they are packed in crates, and shipped to slaughter. Fully conscious turkeys are hung upside down by metal shackles. They suffer from pain, and terror, as they are carried on a conveyor belt. Their throats cut. They are not stunned, and as a result, hens and toms are bled to death while fully conscious. The killing methods are not precise, so many sentient individuals go into tanks of boiling water while still alive.

Foie Gras is produced from hens, drakes and ganders (ducks and geese) who are a few months old. These unfortunate individuals are confined in dark sheds, and force fed large amounts of food several times a day. A worker grabs the hen, drake or gander, and forces a metal pipe down his or her neck. Then a mechanized pump shoots a mixture of corn and oil directly into their throat and stomach. This is done for a few weeks, during which time many birds die from ruptured, punctured throats, burst stomachs, and other ailments. They are dehydrated because they are not given sufficient amounts of water. In addition, they are often debeaked to prevent stressed individuals from injuring each other in unhealthy, crowded conditions.

Debeaking is done by a hot blade cutting through bone, cartilage, and soft tissue without any pain relief. The birds' enlarged livers are sold as a 'gourmet' food item after a horrific slaughter. Foie gras production is banned in the United Kingdom, Austria, Czech Republic, Denmark, Finland, Sweden, Norway, Poland, Switzerland, and Israel. It should be banned in the United States and other nations also.

Cattle, heifers, cows and bulls are often born, and live, on ranches unprotected from inclement weather. Thousands die because ranchers do not think it is economical to provide shelter, or veterinary care to injured, ill or otherwise ailing individuals They have holes punched in their ears for identification tags. These tags have numbers, not names. Cattle are branded with hot irons, which is extremely painful and traumatic. There is no pain relief or infection prevention administered. Cows and bulls are often transported for hundreds or thousands of miles. By law, they are allowed to travel for up to 36 hours without food or water.

Thousands of these individuals die every year from overcrowding, stress and disease. At stockyards and auctions, frightened individuals are kicked or shocked, and sold to the highest bidder. From there they go to slaughter or a feedlot. Younger heifers and bulls spend the last few months of their lives ingesting growth hormones, and being fed an abnormal diet designed to produce fast growth. Unfortunate sick and diseased individuals are common in these filthy places.

Small planes flying over can smell the stench from high above the feedlots. At slaughter, conditions make it nearly impossible to treat the sentient beings with any semblance of dignity. Although cattle are covered by the Human Slaughter Act, it is seldom enforced.

Dairy cows live short, confined lives of repeated rapes by male workers who first put their arm up to the elbow inside the terrified individual's rectum to turn her uterus to prepare for the rape. If conception does not take place, the process is repeated. This is done annually. In addition, these exploited individuals endure unnatural feeds, painful injections, and calcium depleted bones.

To produce milk, dairy cows must give birth. They produce a calf a year, which is taken from them soon after birth. Mother cows mourn the loss of their baby calves. The cows endure a physically demanding nine month gestation period, during which time they give milk for the first seven months. With genetic mutation, cows produce 100 pounds of milk a day – ten times more than in nature. Their udders are so heavy and swollen that they are in constant pain and are unable to walk properly. Hormones banned in Europe and Canada are used in the United States to increase milk production. This causes birth defects in the calves.

The cows are fed unnatural diets which cause disease, some of which are fatal. All dairy cows suffer from diseases directly related to the way they are treated. In nature, cows live about 20 years, in the dairy industry, they are 'unproductive', spent, and slaughtered at about three or four years old. They are slaughtered in horrific ways, and become low grade hamburger, and low quality beef products.

"Downed cows" are worn out, depleted dairy cows who are so weak, and diseased from the lives they have been forced to live, that they cannot stand. These "downers" are still sold for human consumption. They are typically left without food, water, or care, for days until it is convenient to take them to slaughter. Usually they are moved by the most convenient, least humane ways, such as being dragged or pushed with tractors or forklifts. This causes even more suffering and injuries. Downed animals are not protected from abuse under federal animal welfare laws, no matter how cruel the treatment is.

Veal calves are the by-product of the dairy industry. Male calves are not able to produce milk, so they are taken from their mothers, chained by the neck, and kept in crates so small they cannot turn around, stretch, or lie down. Their muscles are not able to develop, keeping their meat 'tender'. They are fed a poor diet, making them anemic. These sick, abused animals produce pale-colored flesh. These inhumane conditions cause the calves to be more likely to develop diseases than cattle in more normal circumstances. Veal calves requires copious amounts of medication to keep them alive until slaughter at a few months of age. Veal is the most likely meat to contain illegal drug residues which pose a threat to human consumption.

Sows, Boars and Piglets. Approximately 100 million pigs are raised and slaughtered in the United States every year. In nature, pigs live in social groups in light woodlands. They are as intelligent as dogs, naturally very clean, and are very active. Pigs are one of the most intelligent and affectionate animals on earth. Pregnant sows build large nests where they give birth and protect their piglets. The piglets are weaned in nature from milk to solid food at 10 – 20 weeks.

Undercover investigations reveal that when these docile, loving creatures are raised for food they are subjected to the most egregious abuses imaginable. For example, semen is collected from the boars (male pigs) by means that should be considered beastiality.

The sows (female pigs) are locked in cages so small that they cannot stand or turn around. They are immobilized like this for their entire short lives. Even in prison solitary confinement, prisoners can stand and walk. And the sows have done nothing wrong to deserve this!

In this vulnerable position, from which there is no escape, the docile, intelligent, sentient girls are artificially inseminated by workers. These cruel men manipulate the sows' vaginas to insert the semen. Sometimes a boar (male pig), is dragged around by a robot between forced masturbation sessions in the hope that this poor unfortunate's smell will facilitate the heinous procedure. The sweet, gentle sows are then raped repeatedly until conception takes place.

Of all pigs, the breeding sows are treated the most cruelly. They live in a continual cycle of artificial insemination from masturbated male pigs, birth, and re-impregnation. The sows are confined in small, metal gestation crates. For their entire lives, the sows cannot walk or turn around, and barely have room to stand up. They are denied straw bedding and must lie on concrete.

When the innocent baby pigs are born, they nurse from their incarcerated, pinned down Mothers briefly before being removed by workers. In factory farms, piglets are taken from their grieving Mothers when they are as young as three weeks old. The Mother's and Babies' screams are heartbreaking. The Mothers mourn the loss of their babies, as any other mother would. Their physical, and psychological suffering is immense.

The baby piglets are housed in indoor barren, over-crowded pens. There is no straw or other bedding. They lie on concrete. After piglets are taken from their mothers, their tails are cut off with pliers, or a hot docking iron, without pain relief causing permanent pain. The baby boy piglets have their testicles removed without anesthesia or pain relief. Their high-pitched screams are heart breaking. They also have their tails removed to prevent the natural act of sucking by their companions looking for mother's milk. Their teeth are filed down to prevent 'financial loss' from cannibalism caused by the unbearable circumstances of their short lives. The mutilations cause pain, illness, and even death.

Approximately 15% of the piglets die soon after leaving their mothers. The surviving piglets endure horrific circumstances until their death at six months of age after they have gained weight.

Each sow is forced to have 20 piglets per year. After three or four years, the breeding sows are no longer deemed productive, and are sent to slaughter. Slaughter/murder comes for the Mothers when they are no longer able to produce babies either because their reproductive organs have been expelled from their bodies, or they have become so hopeless that they stop eating.

All this horror these gentle individuals are forced to endure is so someone can 'enjoy' ham or bacon. It is not worth it.

Fish caught in the wild are killed in the most horrific, inhumane ways. Often nets that are miles long are used. These nets catch and kill many untargeted individual fish, who are just in the wrong place, at the wrong time. There are no regulations to insure humane treatment of fish. Fish plants in the

U.S. make no effort to stun fish. Fish are completely conscious when they are cut. They convulse in pain as they die.

With oceans becoming exhausted, more than 40% of all fish consumed each year are now raised on aqua farms. These fish spend their entire lives in cramped, filthy enclosures. They suffer from parasites, diseases, and injuries. The United Nations Food and Agriculture Organization (UNFAO) reports that the aquaculture industry is growing three times faster than land-based animal agriculture.

Deformities and stress related injuries are common, and as many as 40% of the farmed fish are blind due to the horrific conditions they are raised in. Because they are designed to navigate vast oceans using all their senses, they go insane from cramped conditions, and lack of space. Salmon farms are intensely crowded with as many as 50,000 individuals in an enclosure.

Lobsters carry their young for nine months, and can live 100 years. Researcher Michael Kuba says that lobsters are "amazingly smart." They establish social relationships, and take long-distance seasonal journeys of 100 miles or more each year. When kept in tanks, they suffer from the stress of confinement, low oxygen levels, and crowding.

Neurobiologist Tom Abrams says that lobsters have "a full array of senses." Lobsters may feel even more pain than we would in similar situations.

According to Invertebrate Zoologist Jaren G. Horsley, "The lobster does not have an autonomic nervous system that puts it into a state of shock when it is harmed. It probably feels itself being cut…I think the lobster is in a great deal of pain from being cut open…and feels all the pain until its nervous system is destroyed during cooking".

Crabs have well-developed senses of sight, smell, and taste. Research indicates that they have the ability to feel pain.
Dr. Robert Elwood, from Queens University in Belfast, who has studied crustaceans for decades, says "Denying that crabs feel pain because they don't have the same biology as mammals is like denying they can't see because they don't have a visual cortex."

Millions of crabs are caught and killed yearly in the United States. With these doomed crabs, are birds, fish, and other marine animals, who are thrown back into the water dead or dying.

Shrimp is perhaps the most popular of all the shellfish. Each one is an individual who had a life and suffers death. They did not volunteer to be someone's dinner or appetizer. They preferred to live a long and happy life with their friends and family, just like everyone else.

Chapter 26
What You Wear Reflects Your Compassion

The Plant-Based Lifestyle involves more than diet. It is about compassion and courage. What we wear reflects our level of compassion. Leather, fur, down, and wool are not compassionate choices. There are many synthetic and faux alternatives available. They are compassionate, practical, affordable and attractive.

Please be mindful of others of all species when choosing clothing. There are many compassionate alternatives available, which are just as affordable and attractive – sometime even more so – then the crueler versions. Additionally, you will be much, much more attractive in these alternatives because the beauty of your compassion and courage will show through more effectively than anything you are wearing.

How many people do you know who would never think of eating meat (and maybe dairy) but love to wear leather? Maybe you wear leather! Here are some facts to consider before you purchase your next leather article.

Leather is a big business. It often involves completely conscious cows, and calves, being skinned alive, or thrown into scalding hot tanks. Slaughterhouse production lines move at breakneck speeds, so workers routinely skin and dismember fully conscious animals to produce leather.

Much of the leather sold in the U.S. comes from India, where the leather trade is perhaps the cruelest in the world. Workers beat and torture tired, thirsty animals to keep them marching endless miles to slaughter. Most Indian animals used for leather are so sick and injured by the time they arrive at the slaughterhouse that they must be dragged. Many have hot chili peppers, and tobacco rubbed into their eyes. Their tail bones are painfully twisted and broken. This is to force the weak animals into the slaughterhouse. Once inside, their throats are slit. Some have their legs hacked off or are skinned while still alive.

In Asia dogs and cats are cruelly killed for their skin. Dog and cat skins from Asia are used without being labeled as such. They are simply labeled 'leather" and show up in products all over the world.

What about shoes, belts, and handbags? Being leather free can be fashionable. Products abound that are leather free. Markets respond to consumer desires, so more choices are constantly becoming available as we shop for them. If your taste is designer quality, consider Stella McCartney, daughter of Sir Paul McCartney, and one of the world's top designers. She makes designer leather free items.

When I shop, I often ask salespeople if a handbag is leather. I make sure they are aware I want a cruelty-free product. Their response is always positive as they assure me no animals were hurt to make this product. Recently I purchased a purse designed by Kenneth Cole. The label read,

"Genuine Non-Leather". I bought it in an instant!

Snakes captured in Asia are inflated with compressed air while still alive, then skinned and disemboweled for fancy shoes and bags. I would rather be barefoot and carrying my things in my hands than support that!

Fur comes from animal such as foxes, minks, rabbits and others, who live their lives in cruel confinement. Then they are anally or vaginally electrocuted or bludgeoned to death. Fur continues to become less popular and I hope you will help continue that trend!

Down involves pulling the feathers out of ducks and geese and leaving them bleeding and suffering. Many do not survive the ordeal. These are not feathers that fell off the birds and were gathered from the ground as some people believe. There are terrific, warm, luxurious down-alternatives available. Please try them.

Wool. Sheep are docile, gentle animals who feel pain, fear, and loneliness. If not genetically manipulated, they would grow just enough wool to protect themselves from temperature extremes. Their fleece provides insulation from cold and heat.

Shearers are paid by volume, not by the hour, which encourages them to work quickly without any regard for the welfare of the sheep. Their carelessness leads to frequent injuries. Large wounds are sewn with needle and threat, and no pain relief. Strips of skin, teats, tail, and ears are often carelessly cut off during shearing. Sheep are punched, kicked, and stomped on, and hit in the face with electric clippers while being sheared. Workers stand on the sheep's heads, necks, and hind legs. One shearer was seen hitting a lamb on the head with a hammer. Another used a sheep's body to wipe her own urine off the floor. Another shearer repeatedly twisted, and bent a sheep's neck, breaking it. In one case, a sheep died, was roasted, and eaten, by workers in full view of the other sheep, who knew what was going on.

A commonly used process called 'mulesing" involves cutting huge chunks of skin from the sheep's' backside without painkillers. Within weeks of birth, lambs' ears are hole punched, their tails chopped off, and males are castrated without painkillers. Male lambs are castrated between 2 and 8 weeks old, either by making an incision, and cutting their testicles off, or with a rubber ring used to cut off blood supply – one of the most painful methods of castration possible. If the lamb's testicles do not fall off, they are cut off with clippers. Every year, hundreds of lambs die before the age of 8 weeks from exposure or starvation. Mature sheep die every year from disease, lack of shelter, and neglect.

Unwanted Australian sheep are shipped to the Middle East on crowded multilevel ships. These voyages can last for weeks. There is no food or water available for the sheep. In summer months, the sheep literally cook to death. They are surrounded by their deceased friends and family members. Urine and feces are not removed until after the months long voyage. When they arrive at the 'gates of hell' as someone once put it, they are dragged by their ears or legs, and slaughtered while still conscious.

Standards and humane laws are nonexistent.

Corporations, benefactors of the dramatic shift of power in the world today, are being held accountable for their actions. One such example is Emanuel Exports, Australia's largest live sheep exporter.

Emanuel Exports recently had its license revoked. After sheep are no longer considered profitable, they are shipped alive. More than 100,000 liters of urine and feces accumulates on a typical live export ship every day during the weeks that the sheep are on board. The ship won't be 'washed out' until after they disembark. There is no food or water for the animals, and heat makes on-board conditions catastrophic. When temperatures soar, sheep are literally cooked alive. Any live animal needing to lie down risks being buried in excrement. Those who survive will continue to suffer, now surrounded by the dead bodies of their companions.

Heavily pregnant ewes are shipped for slaughter like every other animal. They will endure the trauma of live export while going into labor and giving birth. Babies born on live export ships will lose their mothers, be trampled, or be killed by distressed crew members who are routinely ordered to slit the babies' throats. Weeks later, when they arrive in the Middle East, those individuals remaining alive will be slaughtered in the most horrific ways imaginable, such as 'halal'. All this is after enduring a lifetime of suffering while being raised for wool.

Please consider that an important part of your transition to a Plant-Based Lifestyle involves not just your diet and health, but also the well-being of others, and make the decisions necessary to implement this in your new healthful and happy Lifestyle. Remember, you cannot be happy while making others unhappy. The individuals in these scenarios are much more than just unhappy! Increase your happiness by not adding to their misery.

Chapter 27 Entertainment

The Plant-Based Lifestyle includes choice of entertainment. There are plenty of good shows and animal free entertainment. There are even animal free circuses. Please patronize these and not the non-compassionate choices.

Animals used for entertainment in circuses, rodeos, zoos, aquariums, and seaquariums lead completely unnatural lives. There is nothing compassionate about being entertained by a captive orca. Tilikum, an orca, was featured in the documentary "Blackfish". He was not alone. Lolita, another popular orca, has languished for nearly 50 years in Miami in the smallest tank in North America. Orcas are social animals like elephants. Like many other orcas, Lolita has not had the companionship of family, friends, or any other orcas in nearly 50 years. Her only companion for a brief while committed suicide from the stress of confinement.

Zoos, pseudo-sanctuaries, traveling shows, and roadside displays use animals who are forced to spend their lives behind bars just to entertain the public. These animals live completely unnatural lives. Their living conditions are usually dismal, with animals confined to filthy, barren enclosures. Even the best environments can't come close to matching the freedom that animals want and need. Animals are bored, lonely, and often abused by their caregivers. The symptoms of their suffering are rocking, swaying, pacing endlessly, and hurting themselves.

Circuses are another cruel choice in entertainment. Animals in circuses are not volunteers or paid employees. They are beaten, shocked with electric prods or small hand-held easily concealed devices, chained, and whipped to make them perform unnatural and often dangerous tricks. Bullhooks, long sticks with sharp metal hooks, are used to intimidate and

'discipline' elephants. Elephants, big cats, bears, horses, and primates are beaten with sticks, axe handles, baseball bats, and metal pipes in order to break their spirits, and show them 'who's boss'.

Whips are used violently in training and cause lingering, intense pain. They are used again in performances as a reminder of what is waiting if the animal is unwilling or physically unable to perform correctly. In 2000 in White Plains, New York, an elephant named Petunia was beaten to death by ten trainers, for failing to perform her trick correctly due to advanced, untreated arthritis. This is not an unusual or isolated incident.

Most circus elephants were captured in the wild. Baby elephants born to these traumatized mothers are removed at birth, tied with ropes, and kept in isolation until they learn to fear their trainers. Then they are brutally 'trained' which often leads to death. The mothers grieve inconsolably.

Tigers are naturally afraid of fire. 'Training' tigers so severely traumatizes them that they are willing to jump through hoops of fire. Tigers can become caught in these hoops and suffer severe burns - if they survive.

Big cats, bears, primates, and other animals are forced to eat, drink, sleep, defecate, and urinate in the same cramped cages. They are often transported around the country in the worst conditions. A young tiger named Clyde died from heat while being transported though the Mohave dessert. His train car where he literally cooked to death, was not checked by circus personnel for days.

There are many animal free circuses in the United States. Children can have fun without causing animals to suffer.

Rodeos are not compassionate. Animals used in rodeos are not aggressive by nature. Without the use of spurs, tail twisting, and bucking straps cinched tightly around their abdomen and groin, these frightened, and often docile animals would not 'buck'.

Bulls and horses are tormented in the chutes prior to being released into the ring. The animals are terrorized into action when these 'brave' cowboys and cowgirls shove electric prods into them, twist their necks, yank them by their tails or legs, slam them to the ground, and otherwise batter them.

Injuries to these animals include deep internal organ bruising, hemorrhaging, bone fractures, ripped tendons, torn ligaments and muscles. The animals are used repeatedly before finally being sent to slaughter. They arrive at slaughterhouses so extensively bruised that often the only areas in which the skin is attached to the body is the head, neck, legs and belly. Rodeo animals can have as many as six or eight broken ribs protruding from the spine, often puncturing their lungs. It is not uncommon for there to be two or three gallons of free blood accumulated under the detached skin. Inspectors in slaughterhouses say the rodeo animals are in the worst condition they have ever seen.

Animal racing is not like athletic racing. Horses and dogs do not decide to race the way human athletes do. Instead, first they are breed through horrific methods. Mares (female horses) are immobilized using painful devices. Then a group of ten men forces the stallion (male horse) on the mare. No matter how much the stallion refuses, he cannot escape from the ten men. Stallions are used like this hundreds of times during a breeding season for steep stud fees. The female is impregnated repeatedly in search of the perfect offspring who can win races and enrich their owners. The colts who show promise are subjected to many brutal, often life-threatening techniques, to enhance performance. The many, many horses who do not make the grade are eliminated in the most horrific ways. Horses don't bet on humans; humans shouldn't bet on horses.

Dogs, specifically greyhounds, used in racing are killed when they don't show promise for a racing career. Those who do race are killed when they no longer produce a profit. They are shot, bludgeoned, or euthanized. One track in Florida kills approximately 600 to 800 dogs yearly. Greyhounds are characteristically gentle and undemanding. They seldom bite no matter what pain or indignities are inflicted on them.

Horse-drawn carriages are often struck by vehicles resulting in severe injuries or death to horses, drivers, passengers, and others. Horses can become frightened, and race into traffic or onto sidewalks. Often veterinary care is refused by carriage owners for horses' injuries. Horses are subjected to blistering heat and humidity, hot and hard pavement, traffic congestion, exhaust fumes, constant exposure to sun, long hours, inadequate rest, and are given little or no water. Their lives are jeopardized when they cannot cool themselves. Pavement temperature is often 50 degrees hotter than air. Horses enslaved by the carriage industry usually return from a treacherous day's work to a filthy hard floor without clean bedding, no access to pasture, and inadequate food and water. They are often malnourished. They are prevented from socializing with each other, and often tied to poles.

Chapter 28 Experiments

Animal experiments are outdated and cruel. There are models available which more closely, and accurately, represent the human body, and do not cause unnecessary and cruel suffering to animals in labs. Because of physiological variations between species, human reactions to drugs differ from those of animals.

Millions of rabbits, guinea pigs, rats and other mammals are force-fed cosmetics and household products. This results in convulsions, vomiting, and bleeding from the eyes, nose, mouth, and even death. Animals cower in fear in barren cages, often causing them to self-mutilate. Cages have been put through automatic washing machines while the animals are still in them. This carelessness scalds them to death. Dogs and cats who were formerly household pets are procured from Class B Dealers. These former pets often still have their collars on during painful, often deadly experiments. The only interaction lab animals have with humans is when they are restrained so that painful procedures can be performed, or when they are euthanized.

Baby chimps are taken at birth from their mothers. These mothers have been constrained at the neck, wrists, waist, and ankles, immobilizing them with their legs spread apart, on the so called 'rape rack'. The female chimps are repeatedly artificially inseminated by male lab workers to cause conception. The baby chimps, and their mothers, never experience a single act of kindness during their sometimes 30 years of life. The baby chimps' grow up constantly having blood drawn, being infected with various deadly diseases, and then are categorized as DNR – do not resuscitate.

Chapter 29 Drugs

A Plant-Based Lifestyle requires that we eat cruelty free food, wear cruelty free clothing, patronize cruelty free entertainment, use cruelty free products, and cruelty free drugs.

Premarin is the ultimate in cruelty and can often cause severe side effects in the women who use it. Premarin stands for PREgnant MAREs urINe, or pregnant mare's urine. Mares (female horses) are artificially inseminated, forced to stand in stalls so small that they cannot lie down, or turn around. Cups are attached to their bodies to catch their urine. Water is restricted, causing the pregnant mares to be dehydrated when their body most needs water. This unhealthy, cruel treatment produces urine which is highly concentrated with hormones. When the baby colt is born, he or she is removed, and killed as an unwanted byproduct of the drug industry. The poor mare who just lost her baby is impregnated again - if she is still standing. If not, she is also killed after a life of unbearable physical and emotional misery.

The purpose of this drug is to relieve symptoms of menopause in women. It has caused serious physical problems in women who are taking it. Plant-Based women do not use premarin or hormone replacement therapy (HRT) because they do not need it. Soy mimics estrogen in women's bodies. Menopausal symptoms can be relieved by eating a little tofu. There are no adverse effects to men or boys from eating soy.

In addition, for relief of menopausal symptoms, there are cruelty free products such as Estriol-Care, and Natural Progesterone Cream. There are also bioidentical hormones synthetically produced in Labs from plant sources. These possess the same molecular structure as natural hormones. Dietary phytoestrogens are naturally occurring substances found in fruits, vegetables, and whole grains such as soy beans and alfalfa sprouts, and oil seeds such as flax seeds, which also reduce the intensity and frequency of hot flashes.

Chapter 30
My Plant-Based Vegan Kitchen

Any book about food would be remiss without a tour of the Author's kitchen. So here it is!

Utensils. There was no change in any utensils when changing from the old fashioned meat and dairy based diet to vegan cuisine 20 plus years ago. I use the same knives, wooden spoons, spatula, scraper, etc. In fact, the instrument I use to turn corn on the cob over under the broiler is the same instrument that my parents used to remove my baby bottles from hot water (no comment on how many years ago). Although it does not seem like knives are necessary for a Plant-Based Lifestyle, I challenge you to try to tackle a butternut squash without a chainsaw!

The Basics. My goal is to use only Veganic produce, hopefully from my own farm someday. For now, I buy fruit, berries, and vegetables from a local produce market. Usually I know what I want, like bananas, blueberries, and corn on the cob. But I am also open to surprises and whatever is fresh and attractive. In addition, I buy rice (brown, jasmine, basmati, wild, etc) depending on what is available, and what I am in the mood for. I also include lentils, split peas, chic- peas, pinto beans, black beans, etc.

Measure. I do not measure anything except oatmeal. Sorry if that is a disappointment. I usually 'wing it', and everything turns out just fine.

Oil. I use canola oil cooking spray for sauteing, but I know many people saute in water. I do not use oil for salad or anything else except Massage (oil for receiving Massage, not eating).

Vegan Food Products. I purchase Follow Your Heart Vegenaise. I have tried Hellman's Vegan Mayo, which was delicious, but I have not seen it again. I use this with a little balsamic vinegar to make cole slaw from shredded cabbage or macaroni salad from pasta. It is so good!

Plant milk. Oat, almond, soy, whatever, is delicious - and good in coffee.

Plant butter. For broiled corn on the cob etc.

Egg Substitute. For vegan cakes I use a teaspoon of clear vinegar and enough plant milk to make ¼ cup to replace one egg. It works beautifully. Everyone loves my imaginative and festive vegan holiday cakes. When my Grandchildren were small, they would only eat Grandma's vegan cakes for dessert on holidays, no matter how beautiful the store bought desserts were! They don't do that anymore.

I had humble beginnings, and live and eat simply. Although I am completely at home at black tie events, parties in Sutton Place, the Indonesian Lounge at the United Nations, and other upscale and exotic venues, talking to United States Senators, United Nations Ambassadors, Celebrities, and more, I stay true to my humble roots at home.

Please enjoy your plant-based lifestyle experience in whatever way makes you happy. Vegan is about compassion - to yourself and others of all species! Remember if you are eating out – many vegetarian options contain milk and butter. Be careful. Most importantly – enjoy yourself!

Chapter 31
Forgiveness and Happiness

Lifestyle includes not only compassionate choices in diet, entertainment, clothing, products, drugs, exercise, relaxation, detox, but also courage, happiness, and forgiveness.

A Plant-Based Lifestyle may seem at times to be all about what you can't have or can't do. This may feel like depravation compared to the hedonistic lifestyles of others. Are they really happy? Are you really unhappy? I don't think so.

"Most folks are about as happy as they make their minds up to be." This famous quote was attributed to President Abraham Lincoln in 1914, fifty years after his death as part of a column in the Syracuse Herald written by Dr. Frank Crane. Unfortunately, no evidence exists to suggest that the popular and valid quote really was from the greatest American orator. I like it anyway. It is true for the Plant-Based crowd as well as everyone else.

Further, here is a bit of wisdom I found in a store in Locust Valley, Long Island years ago, and it has stayed with me ever since because of its enormous wisdom: "Happiness lies not in having what you want, but in wanting what you have." I love this quote and tell it to myself whenever necessary.

Forgiveness is something most of us would rather not think about. It somehow does not seem relevant in our busy, productive lives. However, I do not believe that the human body can be truly healthy if it is holding on to the negative emotion of unforgiveness. Resolving the situation is not something you do because you have to. You do it because you want to free yourself of the negativity of unforgiveness that has the potential to hurt you, not whoever caused the original, probably long gone original issue. This is the only way to be truly healthy.

Recently I had the fortuitous opportunity of experiencing a life-threatening situation! After two years and eight Doctors, something the size of walnut was removed from my neck. Had it remained, it could have pressed against my carotid artery, effectively cutting of the blood supply to my brain, and kill me! Whew! Glad that's over! I was lucky enough to choose a surgeon who refused to follow the orders of the Pathologist in the Operating Room who wanted him to remove my lymph nodes. Dr. Ellis L. Webster, my Surgeon, and currently the Premier of the British Overseas Territory of Anguilla, knew I was not a candidate for cancer. He was right. Who knew things were about to get even better!

Somehow after the life-saving surgery, a nerve and a vocal cord in my neck touched. There is a lot going on in a relatively small space in necks. There are the nerves going to and from the brain, muscles supporting the head, air going between the lungs and nose, and food traveling from the mouth to the rest of the digestive system. It is a busy little area!

My voice was gone! I always thought eyes were the most important part of the body – until I tried life without a voice. This was so much more devastating than I could have ever imagined!

I needed my voice! I had so many plans which were much easier to accomplish in person than in writing. Like anyone else, I was willing to do anything to get what I wanted. It started with not accepting being placated on the phone with my wispy, barely audible raspy sound - that it would get better. I insisted on an in-person appointment. It turned out my choice was 'wait and see if it gets better', or additional surgery.

Due to a variety of reasons, I had to wait almost a month for the surgery appointment. During that time, I tried almost anything I could think of to try to insure its success. This consisted of not only a variety of Prayer Lists, but also a Healing Mass, and something sponsored by the Diocese of Palm Beach called "Unbound". I was willing to do or try anything.

"Unbound" consists of five "keys". The first is Forgiveness. Forgiveness, what a concept! Yes, we have all heard of it, even tried it. However, there is no comparison between trying it, and doing it because you are concerned that something you value intensely may depend on it. I could not take a chance of possibly loosing something I really wanted – my voice. I was willing to try anything, even forgiveness.

Cori Ten Bloom comes to mind as a giant of Forgiveness. She and her family were part of the World War II Dutch Resistance. They hid fugitives and participated in other clandestine activities. Yes, they were caught, and interned in the camps.

Cori was from a big family. Her favorite sister perished because of the harsh conditions of the camps. Prior to her death, Cori's sister had been tortured and abused by a guard.

After the War, Cori promoted Forgiveness in Churches and other venues. On one occasion, she invited her audience to come forward for a hug. In the line was the guard who had abused her favorite sister.

Although I was always inspired by the true story of Cori Ten Bloom embracing and forgiving this guard, my current situation gave even more urgency to learning this lesson. At that point in my life, I wanted my voice back even more than I wanted anything else - even resisting forgiving. I forgave everyone who had ever hurt me totally and unconditionally.

The surgery was today. No, I still don't know if I will get my voice back. The Doctor wants me to wait three days before speaking. But from the few 'mistakes' I made it sounds like there is a voice!

This was written a few years ago. There have been many more challenges, but one thing never changes, no matter what it is, forgiveness is always the best policy.

"Forgiveness is an act of the will, and the will can function regardless of the temperature of the heart." Cornelia Arnolda Johanna "Corrie" ten Boom

Chapter 32 Conclusion

Kindness trumps smart any day!

The plant-based (vegan) lifestyle has a much broader scope than just diet, health and exercise. It is a Lifestyle in every sense of the word: mind, body, and soul. It includes apparel – eliminating leather and wool, etc.; products – shampoos, makeup, cleansers, etc. must be 'cruelty free' which means both 'no animal ingredients' and 'not tested on animals'; drugs must not include ingredients from animals: lanoline, lactic acid, etc., or be from animal cruelty such as Premarin (pregnant mare's urine); and the intangibles of kindness, courage, compassion, determination and happiness.

It requires courage to pursue this path, and determination not to give up when others around you do not act compassionately. It involves not only people, the planet, and our fellow travelers on Spaceship Earth, but also the broader concepts of Peace, Prosperity, and Social Justice.

It is my belief that Peace, Prosperity, and Social Justice will be impossible to attain while the results of extreme violence are in the bodies of the world's population. Sentient beings and what is unjustly taken from their bodies, eaten and digested by humans - the products of violence - nourish every cell of those humans' bodies through the digestive process. How is it possible, under those circumstances, to accomplish something which is totally opposite of what permeates the entire body? There is a proven correlation between animal abuse and other, more aggressive violence, towards people. Mahatma Gandhi believed eating meat causes violence, even wars. Promoting the Plant-Based Vegan Lifestyle may be one of the greatest contributors to Peace, Justice, Prosperity and to protecting our home, planet Earth.

Pride is considered the deadliest of the capital sins. Could it be pride that prevents people from living a compassionate plantbased lifestyle? Do people think it is okay to eat and exploit animals because humans are 'better' than other sentient individuals, or that these others don't 'count' because they cannot talk or do not accumulate money? In Proverbs 29:23, the Bible warns that a man's pride will bring him low. Maybe that is what we are seeing now with the zoonotic pandemics, preventable diseases, climate change, and countless other issues.

By now I hope it is clear that the meat and dairy based diet equals death. Death from preventable disease for affluent humans, death from hunger and starvation for vulnerable humans, death from slaughter and exploitation for non-humans, and death for our home, spaceship Earth, from climate change, pollution, and destruction of scarce resources. The plant-based diet is just the opposite. It represents life for humans, nonhumans, and spaceship Earth.

Lifestyle, however, is about choices. You can choose to be inconsiderate or compassionate, responsible or not, whatever you want to choose. I suggest that you choose life.

Deuteronomy 30:19
"This day I call the heavens and the earth as witnesses that I have set before you life and death, blessings and curses. Now choose life so that you and your children may live."

Enjoy your Transition to a new Plant-Based Lifestyle. It is easy, fun, delicious and healthful!

Resources

Introduction: Contributing Writer Marilyn Pocius, "Vegan Bible"; American Dietetic Association; Dean Ornish, M.D., "Dr. Dean Ornish's Program"

Chapter 1 Nutrition 101: Neal Barnard, M.D.; John McCabe, Sunfood Traveler; John A. McDougall, M.D. "The McDougal Program; Neal Barnard, M.D., "The Vegan Starter Kit"; "The Raw Cure Healing Beyond Medicine" by Jesse Jacoby, Sharon L. Wallenberg, Nutritionist.

Chapter 2 Chapter 2 Digestion: Carla Money "Inside the Human Body", Anne Wanjie "The Basics of the Human Body", Reader's Digest, "ABC's of the Human Body A Family Answer Book", Sharon L. Wallenberg, Nutritionist and Licensed Colon Therapist.

Chapter 3 Raw Foods: Jennifer Cornbleet, "Raw Food Made Easy", Sharon L. Wallenberg, Nutritionist.

Chapter 4 Water: F. Batmanghelidj, M.D.,

"Your Body's Many Cries For Water"; John A. McDougal, M.D., "The McDougall Program; Sharon L. Wallenberg (research on water while working for Kangen Water Filters).

Chapter 5 Rejuvenation and Detoxification: Sharon L. Wallenberg, Licensed Esthetician and Massage Therapist; Dr. Tiffany Field, the University Miami School of Medicine, Touch Research Institute; Hans Selig.

Chapter 6 Exercise: Neal Barnard, M.D., "Why Are Athletes Racing To A Vegan Diet", Robert Cheeke, Torre Washington, Mac Danzig.

Chapter 7 Preventing and Reversing Heart Disease: National Institute of Health, Office of Science Policy: The Framingham Heart Study: Laying the Foundation For Preventative Health Care; Dean Ornish, M.D., study published in "The Lancet", Caldwell B. Esselstyn, Jr., M.D., "Prevent and Reverse Heart Disease"; Dean Ornish, M.D., "Dr. Dean Ornish's Program For Reversing Heart Disease"; New England

Journal of Medicine; American Heart Association; National Cholesterol Education Program; National Research Council.

Chapter 8 Understanding Diabetes: Neal Barnard, M.D., Dr. Neal Barnard's Program for Reversing Diabetes"; T. Colin Campbell, Ph.D., Thomas M. Campbell II, M.D., "The China Study – Revised and Expanded"; New
England Journal of Medicine; American Academy of Pediatrics; National Institute of Health; Preventative Medicine; American Journal of Medicine; American Diabetes Association Scientific meeting (2004); American Diabetic Association; American Association of Diabetes Educators; and American Public Health Association (2005-6).

Chapter 9 Combating Cancer: World Cancer Research Fund and the American Institute of Cancer Research, 1977, "Food, Nutrition and the Prevention of Cancer: A Global Perspective"; Nurses' Study, Harvard 1997; Michael Klaper, M.D., "Meat and Cancer"; World Health Organization; International Agency for Research on Cancer (IARC); Neal Barnard, M.D., "The Vegan Starter Kit"; Women's Intervention Nutrition Study (WINS); Women's Healthy Eating and Living (WHEL); Physicians' Health Study; Health Professionals Followup Study; William Harris, M.D., "Cancer and Vegan Diet".

Chapter 10: Hormones and Autoimmune Disease: Neal Barnard, M.D., "Foods That Fight Pain", Neal Barnard, M.D., "Your Body In Balance The New Science of Food, Hormones, and Health"; T. Colin Campbell, Ph.D., The New Science of Food, Hormones, and Health"; T. Colin Campbell, Ph.D. "The China Study"; John McDougall, M.D. "The McDougall Program"; Jenifer Cornbleet, "The Raw Cure".

Chapter 11 Zoonotic Disease: Vegan International Newsletters; The Lancet; Live Science; Zoonoses, Stephen S. Morse et al, The Lancet; Zoonotic Diseases, CDC; WHO/FAO/OIE Report of the Joint

Consultation on Emerging Zoonotic Diseases; Aysha Akhtar, Animals and Public Health Why Treating Animals Better is
Critical To Human Welfare; Center of the Deadly Coronavirus Outbreak, Time Magazine; WHO, H5N1 Avian Influenza: Time-line of major events; Future Medicine; the Center for Disease Control and Prevention (CDC); World Health Organization (WHO); United Nations Food and Agriculture Organization (FAO).

Foedke, Ph.D., Sustainable Energy for All (SE4All), Nigeria; Mahatma Ghandi.

Chapter 15 Chapter Climate Change and You: Vegan International; PETA; Victor Foedke, Sustainable Energy For All, Nigeria; United Nations Climate Ambition Summit; United Nations (UN) Department of Public Information (DPI) NonGovernmental Organization (NGO) Conference on Climate Change; United Nations (UN) Food and Agriculture Organization (FAO) report, 'Livestock's Long Shadow'; UN System Standing Committee on Nutrition (UNSCN);

Chapter 16 From 'Livestock's Long Shadow - Environmental Issues and Options': UN Food and Agriculture Organization (FAO)

Chapter 17 Sustainable Use of Resources and the SDGs: United States Environmental Protection Agency (US EPA); United Nations Sustainable Development Goals (SDGs); Vegan International.

Chapter 18 Effects of Animal

Exploitation on the Human Population and the Environment: PETA; Vegan International.

Chapter 19 Today's Shoah: Alex Hershaft; Charles Patterson, "Eternal Treblinka"; Isaac Bashevis Singer

Chapter 20 United Nations Convention Against Speciesism: Vegan International; Albert Schweitzer.

Chapter 21 Agriculture: Conventional, Organic and Veganic: Mona Seymour, Associate Professor of Urban and Environmental Studies, Loyola Marymount University; Sharon L. Wallenberg, Graduate of the Organic Growers School;

Chapter 22 Chapter 22 Politics of Food: Columbia University School of International and Public Affairs; "Removing the Meat Subsidy: Our Cognitive Dissonance Around Animal Agriculture" by Christina Sewell; David Simon "Meatonomics"; Summary Report: World Agriculture: Towards 2015/2030. Food and Agriculture

Organization of the UN, 2002; Hamblin, James. 2017. "The Environmental Case for a Meat Tax." The Atlantic. December 15, 2017; Worm, Boris, Edward B. Barbier, Nicola Beaumont, J. Emmett Duffy, Carl Folke, Benjamin S. Halpern, Jeremy B. C. Jackson, et al. 2006. "Impacts of Biodiversity Loss on Ocean Ecosystem Services." Science; "Greenhouse Effect 101." Melissa Denchak. n.d. NRDC; "Opinion | The Case for a Carbon Tax on Beef - The New York Times."; "Special Report on the Ocean and Cryosphere in a Changing Climate"; "What Is Ag-Gag Legislation?" ASPCA; "Marco Springmann | Future of Food."

Chapter 23 Dairy Is Scary: John Mc Dougall, M.D., "The Case Against Milk"; Robert Grillo, Founder of Free From Harm, "Farm To Fable"; Animal Recovery Mission (ARM), "Investigation of a Florida Commercial Dairy Farm"; Robert Grillo, Founder of Free From Harm, "I Visited A Small, Organic Dairy Farm to See If

Animals Were Treated Better"; Nassim Nobari, "Seed the Commons calls on the San Francisco Board of Education to take a stance against school milk".

Chapter 24 The Truth About Eggs: Free From Harm; PETA.

Chapter 25 What We Eat Shows Our Courage and Compassion PETA, United Nations Food and Agriculture Organization, UNFAO; Researcher Michael Kuba; Neurobiologist Tom Abrams; Invertebrate Zoologist Jaren G. Horsley; Dr. Robert Elwood, Queens University, Belfast.

Chapter 26 What You Wear Reflects Your Compassion PETA; Animals Australia.

Chapter 27 Entertainment PETA; "Blackfish";

Chapter 28 Experiments Physicians Committee For Responsible Medicine, (PCRM); PETA;

Chapter 29 Drugs Neal Barnard, M.D., "Your Body In Balance The New Science of

Food, Hormones, and Health"; Physicians Committee For Responsible Medicine (PCRM); PETA.

About The Author: Ms. Wallenberg is the Founder of Vegan

International, a UN ECOSOC NGO applicant (www,VeganInternational.org), Sole Proprietor of Vegan Retreat which offers virtual lectures as well as individual counseling sessions on the plant-based lifestyle (www.VeganRetreat.Life).She is a Health Care Provider with experience as a Dietitian, Licensed Massage Therapist, Colon Therapist, and Esthetician; is certified in Reiki, Reflexology,

Live Blood Cell Analysis, Lymphatic Drainage, and Microdermabrasion; completed the Organic Growers School; member of the Carolina Farm Stewardship Association; and had a Vegan Retreat and Veganic Farm in North Carolina.

Ms. Wallenberg has an MBA from Long Island University; studied Economics on the Doctoral level at Fordham University; has a BA in Business; and Degree in Nutrition.

Ms. Wallenberg is the Author of "The Search For Raoul Wallenberg -The Truth", based on her extensive work on behalf of Raoul Wallenberg, who is credited with saving 100,000 innocent lives during World War II. It tells the story of Mr. Wallenberg's mission, his disappearance, the search for him, and carrying his legacy into the present and future by promoting compassionate choices and lifestyles. www.RaoulWallenbergSearch.com